eat — or be eaten!

Jungle Warfare for the Master Corporate Politician

By Phil Porter

PRENTICE HALL PRESS

Library of Congress Cataloging-in-Publication Data

Porter, Phil.
    Eat—or be eaten:jungle warfare for the master corporate politican/by Phil Porter.
    p. cm.
   ISBN 0-7352-0143-9
    1. Office politics. 2. Executives. 3. Vocational guidance. 1. Title.
HF5386.5.P67 2000
650-1'3—dc21
                                          00-022348

Printed in the United States of America

10 9 8 7 6 5 4 3 2 1

ISBN 0-7352-0143-9

ATTENTION: CORPORATIONS AND SCHOOLS

Prentice Hall books are available at quantity discounts with bulk purchase for educational, business, or sales promotional use. For information, please write to: Prentice Hall Special Sales, 240 Frisch Court, Paramus, New Jersey 07652. Please supply: title of book, ISBN, quantity, how the book will be used, date needed.

PRENTICE HALL PRESS
Paramus, NJ 07652

On the World Wide Web at http://www.phdirect.com

Dedication

This book is possible only due to the personnel departments of all the corporations where I have worked. The term "personnel" is now out of favor. They like to be called human resources, or human-resource-management, or something else. In my mind, these idiots are still the same as they were twenty years ago, with yet a new name. If you can't change the game, and they can't or won't, then change the name.

I want to take this opportunity to thank them for their incompetence, lack of effort on my behalf, and their dearth of diligence toward all the people I have ruined, or seen ruined. When you pray, give thanks to the idiots in Personnel, without whose help this book would not be possible, or necessary.

A special dedication is to one personnel manager. He was a former military first sergeant, and he treated the employees as if they were meat. You read it right, *meat!* If they didn't measure up, they went right into the grinder. He didn't believe that the officers (management) could do anything wrong, and the troops (employees and subordinates if they got out of line) had nothing to say about it. If they did—meat grinder! I could tolerate this guy because I was one of the officers, and I knew exactly where he stood—I could count on his behavior. He was consistent—he hated meat!

Contents

Introduction

Imagine a game you played as a child. It was called king of the hill, or mountain, and the rules were simple: knock people off the mountain so you could occupy it, and then maintain possession against all comers. People in positions of corporate power are kings of their mountains, and they're simultaneously trying to protect them and take over bigger mountains. This book will provide you with some of the rules and techniques of mountain climbing and siege defense. The higher you rise in any large organization, the less time you will spend on the technical aspects of your job and the more you will spend on the purpose of this book—conquering and survival.

I guess you can tell by the dedication that this is a book about turning your subordinates into meat, or if you are a subordinate (and all of us are to someone), keeping from being tonight's dinner. You're right—this is the real world with no crap to clutter it up, just the facts, ma'am. It will inform you, shock you, and scare you to death. Real world—no varnish. Take your time—you've spent the money to buy this, so get your money's worth. Read it twice, and then reread it yearly for the rest of your life. Take it with you to your grave—who knows what the afterlife is like.

Eat—or Be Eaten! Is the compilation of over thirty years' experience in the corporate environment. Because I treat each tactic separately, it will appear as if I got creamed almost a hundred times in my career. Master Corporate Politicians use more than one tactic on a subordinate at a time, some of the best using ten or more simultaneously. Hence, I do not have more bullet holes in me than a firing-range target—I have experienced a lot of tactics. This book has two purposes.

Eat—or Be Eaten! is designed to give you more knowledge about how the Master Corporate Politicians do things so you have a fighting chance to survive and allow your career to prosper. If your goal is to be something other than just another hamburger patty, then this book may be almost important to you as the Holy Bible itself.

Eat—or Be Eaten! will help you if your objective is to be a Master Corporate Politician. You're right, I am one, and I want to help breed some more of me—some more of me with a few ethics. Master Corporate Politicians rule the corporate jungle, and if you want to be one, this book is like finding a gold mine; it's full of nuggets that teach you how to survive or conquer, or both.

Eat—or Be Eaten! covers over a hundred different tactics that are used by some of the most intelligent men and women on the planet. Some are so important that they are touched on several times from different angles. We cover the unwritten, now written, rules. We discuss how to get your way in almost any situation, what to do when you know failure is imminent, and how to respond to your management. We touch on how to actually fix a failure, how to manage your employees, how to get a raise, and a few dirty tricks. In the final three chapters, we get into the big leagues where you are in management and we discuss how to manage your direct reporting supervisors, or avoid being managed if you are a supervisor.

Management in the *real world* is defined as *eat—or be eaten*. Grind, or be ground. You are either the cook, or the meat. Read and survive, or read and prosper.

chapter 1

It's a Jungle in Here

How does one start a book like this? I had several alternatives but I selected the simplest—I went with the general stuff first. It gets more detailed and dirty as the book progresses. In the final chapters, I get into the meat of the workplace, how Master Corporate Politicians get rid of people. The general works best first because it's a building block for the remainder of the book. You need to know routine tactics before you can move to more sophisticated maneuvers, each more complicated than the preceding. This chapter is pretty tame stuff if you have been in the trenches for a few years; but if you have been too busy to pay attention to the Master Corporate Politicians, you may have missed it. Never get too busy to notice them: their methods; their dress; their approach to problems. Remember, these are the guys who rate you, promote you, and if they wish, grind you into oblivion. Study them and learn the basics.

Rule #1, It's Who You Know

I'll take fifty percent efficiency to get one hundred percent loyalty.

SAMUEL GOLDWYN (1882–1974)

Anybody who has ever worked for a living knows the number one rule of politics is, "It isn't what you know, it's who you know." This is one of the unwritten laws of life that you should accept and take advantage of. Just being good isn't good enough. How many of you have worked for a boss who isn't worth a damn, but he's a friend of the boss and that's that? A lot of you—probably most of you.

Why is this? Most us have a tendency to surround ourselves with people we like. We like people who think as we think, and we like people who like us. We trust people who are part of "our team." I know I would rather have a less competent individual who was loyal than one who walked on water that I couldn't trust. You too?

How do you use this knowledge? If you think a minute, you'll realize what I just said probably applies to you. Well, it also applies to your boss and his boss. So, to apply it, you need to be one of the boss's team. You need to make him think he's a direct descendant of Jesus Christ and can do no wrong. You need to support him even when he's wrong and warn him when you think he is, but still support him. If he says to do something stupid, warn him you think it may be a mistake and tell him in terms he will understand; but if he insists, do it just as he told you to do.

Does he like to play golf? If so, then play golf. If you aren't any good at it, then take lessons and ask him to help you. Does he like to play poker? If so, play with him.

Whatever the boss does, you do. Become a clone and let the boss know you think he's the best at whatever it is he does. He will grow to like you and consider you one of his team.

Being a member of "the team" is hard work. I hate golf, but I've played it. I hate poker because I lose too much, but I've played. I don't like to hunt, but I bought a gun. I became a member of my boss's team, and I've been taken care of. Consider it and, if you do it, you, too, can become a member of the team, and your career will rise with your boss's.

Don't Wear Me Out

Man is a tool-using animal. . . . Without tools he is nothing, with tools he is all.

THOMAS CARLYLE (1795–1881)

Ever hear the expression, "one-horse town"? I'm not sure exactly what it means, but I've heard it used in reference to a small, hole-in-the-wall kind of town that consists solely of a gas station and a stoplight. Professional employees who have only a few tactics could be labeled "one-horse executives." If the only tactic you have is overused, then it's no longer a tactic. This book will give you over one hundred tactics and maneuvers—*use them all!*

Think about tactics in terms of food. I hate leftovers. My wife hates them, and so do my children. I bet you do, too. You know what a leftover is? It's the same thing you had before.

Tactics used over and over develop the flavor of leftovers. How do you fix this? The same way my family does with leftovers—we mix them with other entrees and serve them again.

They don't seem as if they're leftovers and are often better than the first time served.

The message? Use tactics in combination, and mix them up. Do you like to eat lima beans at every meal? How would you like to eat just lima beans three times a day with nothing else? You would blow your brains out, right? Tactics are the same. You must have variety and be willing to work out the details in your mind before you use them. With practice, like riding a bike, you will be able to do it quickly and become proficient.

An American soldier going into battle with just an M-16 is an effective fighting tool. If you add some grenades, rocket launchers, artillery, jet strikes, and B-52 bombing raids, then the soldier is almost unstoppable. Tactics are tools. The more tools you develop and use, the more effective you will become. *MIX IT UP!*

 # Get Social

> *If a man does not make new acquaintance as he advances through life, he will soon find himself left alone. A man, Sir, should keep his friendship in constant repair.*
>
> **SAMUEL JOHNSON** (1709–84)

Have you ever wondered where the Master Corporate Politicians come from? Where does your boss's boss find people to fill the slots above you?

I'll let you in on a little secret: he finds them where he socializes. He finds them because they find him and become his friend. He meets them at the golf club, the country club, the Lion's club, the United Way committee, and anywhere else the boss goes when he's not working.

What does this mean to you, an aspiring Master Corporate Politician? It means that some day you're going to have to change jobs, or be in a position to do so. How are you going to know what's out there and who's out there? You join these clubs and organizations to meet people so when you need something there are lots of people to help you. Like a vampire, the Master Corporate Politician joins everything that will let him or her in. He or she makes friends with everyone and everyone likes him or her—they don't have to work with him or her, so it's easy.

The Master Corporate Politician hires his or her friend's children, promotes his golf a bridge partner's son-in-law, and is willing and able to do the same for any other Master Corporate Politician who may be of use to him or her in the future. When the Master Corporate Politician needs a job for themselves, he or she has a bank account of favors owed, and it's usually no problem getting them cashed. It's the way the system works.

You don't believe me? It's true. The former manager of subcontract management with my employer at that time was hired by the vice president and general manager because they knew each other through the United Way. The director of procurement with my former employer was hired by the vice president of material because he met him at one of the civic clubs. I hired a man because the director of quality asked me to. He was his neighbor. He owes me a favor now, and I'm keeping it in the bank. It's true.

The application of this? Get your butt out of the house on nights and weekends and go join up. Join anything, but join, and participate.

The Diary of Record

The palest ink is better than the best memory.

CHINESE PROVERB

The first thing you'll need to know and understand is that a corporation is a jungle. A jungle is full of animals that would love to eat you, and so is a corporation. The Master Corporate Politician will lie, evade, and turn on you like a trapped rat. Survival is the name of the game, and if they have to kill you to survive, they will.

How do you protect yourself? You do it by maintaining a diary of every conversation, letter, fax, telegram, or anything else that might be useful in the future. Remember John Dean? He survived because of his memory and his notes. The Nixon tapes confirmed everything he said, and he wasn't hauled off to the guillotine and beheaded.

What is a diary? It's a hardbound book with prenumbered pages in which you record anything you want to. It must be hardcover, or at least spiral bound with prenumbered pages—this prevents the unethical from going in and creating history after the fact. If you elect to write a memo on a subject, record the memo number in your book and what the subject was. Anything to do with your professional life must be recorded in the book. It'll save your life.

I've never run into any challenge to my memory of events because everyone knows I document everything. My current boss refers to my diary as "my brains." I have a reputation for being a man who keeps careful records, and there have been several occasions when I've been instructed to "not

6

write it down." But I always do, later. Nothing happens in my professional life without being recorded in my diary.

Why do I do this? As I said earlier, Master Corporate Politicians have very convenient memories and they'll lie through their pearly whites. Don't trust anyone.

I had a boss excommunicated because he was incompetent. I documented his every move, instruction, and order as it pertained to me. When he was trying to lay one of his failures off on me, I went to his boss with my diary—the man was gone before the day was over. If I hadn't done it then it would have been my head lying in that basket, or my career would have taken a quick decline. My boss was in trouble and looking for someone to blame it on. I declined—he died the corporate death. Only the diary saved my life.

One of my former bosses told me he was once subpoenaed to testify in a litigation against his former employer. He carried his diary and answered each question honestly, referring to his diary on each occasion. The court accepted his diary as evidence, and he wasn't prosecuted. His former boss and the other executives went to jail. A diary may be considered legal evidence; ask your lawyer.

How many times have you asked for something from an individual who keeps making promises, yet never performs? Keep a record of it in your diary and, when the world comes to an end, you can prove you tried. He failed, not you.

A diary is recognized as a weapon by the Master Corporate Politician. When you finish one, take it home. If they decide to fire you, your insurance policy—your diary—is safe at home. If you're paranoid, run copies of your diary and take them home daily. A diary is the best weapon to protect yourself against a Master Corporate Politician, an unethical boss, or a situation you're not comfortable with. Keep one and refer back to it each week to refresh your memory. It'll save your life.

If you notice that you are writing less and less in your diary, then perhaps your life is too easy. If there isn't much about which you feel the need to write down, then you are not on the cutting edge of where you should be. Read your diary. Is it filled with all the plots and counterplots that are going on around you? No? Then, you have settled into the backwaters of a career and may never escape. I'm not saying this is bad, but if your goal is to rule the mountain, then you aren't going to get there if you sit in the smooth backwaters. A while back, I sat in the backwaters for about six years of my career, and I loved it. The problem is that I didn't move up, or down—I just sat in the same organizational position. If that's what you want, then you don't need a diary.

 # Perception Is Reality

> *The logic of worldly success rests on a fallacy: the strange error that our perfection depends on the thoughts and opinions and applause of other men! A weird life it is, indeed, to be living always in somebody else's imagination, as if that were the only place in which one could at last become real!*

THOMAS MERTON (1915–68)

Have you ever seen a man or woman who you just knew was important? You'd never seen him or her before in your life, but you could tell just by looking that this person was a honcho. He or she was a hot-shot, barn-burning, fast-track mover who was at the top and climbing higher. Get out of the way, or drop to your knees and worship. You can't put your finger on it, but you either feel an immediate urge to be subservient to this person, or to put your hands around his or her neck and strangle the life out of him or her.

Well, sports fans, I have the answer for you. This person is using a Master Corporate Politician technique. Most senior executives have a routine I call the "perception is reality" routine. It's designed to make you think they're somebody and, without evidence to the contrary, you'll think they are. No one wants to "piss off" a big shot by accident. To play it safe, if a person acts as if she's an executive vice president, it's wise to be cautious until you know for sure.

Titles are not power. A few years ago, I held a senior middle-management position. In that position, I acted as if I were the illegitimate son of the chairman of the board. I occasionally chewed out directors and other members of top management and told them what to do. I did it tactfully, but by acting as if I had power I was able to get it.

Matrix positions are popular today, and I think they'll stay around for a while. For those of you who don't know what a matrix position is, it's a job in which you usually don't have anyone working for you, you have the responsibility to make sure something happens, and you work for two or more bosses. You accomplish your task through the staff of the functional managers. A matrix position offers the best opportunity to practice this tactic, and another technique called The Auction, page 34, which is discussed later in this book.

When you're in a matrix position, your power depends on how much the functional managers allow you to have, or how much you're able to wrest out of their hands. You can run to the top dog in a company and tell him that So And So, a functional manager, is not supporting you; but if you run too many times, the top dog is going to conclude that you're not effective and will replace you. You must operate by sheer wit and cunning.

When people know you're matrix, they'll respond to you based on how they perceive your power level. If you act as if you're headed for the board room and this is only a job to keep you busy until a slot opens, you'll be far more effective than if you're just another one of those stupid whining matrix guys. Your perceived power level is the only weapon you have to motivate the functional managers.

When I was the material program manager for a large aerospace program, I used the perception of power as an effective tool to discharge my responsibilities. I was selected as one of only two men (out of over thirteen hundred) to attend a prestigious after-hours training program that lasted over a year and almost guaranteed the graduate he or she would be a director within ten to fifteen years. I made sure everyone I dealt with knew I was part of this program. As if it were a self-fulfilling prophecy, I had no problems with the functional managers and my program received higher priority than the other programs that were competing for their attention. I got a promotion for my efforts.

Another example of how effective the perception of power is occurred when my company took over another company. As a recognized technical expert in materials management, I was sent in as part of the team to "shape those dummies up." My boss, the director of the team, fired a few senior executives immediately, for good reasons, and the rest of the organization responded to all of us as if we had the to power to fire any of them for any reason. We didn't, but they didn't know that, and we used the power they granted us to our advantage to change the culture of the entire organization. We all acted as if we were big shots and by doing so reduced the time to shape up the dummies from the three years it was expected to take to a little over a year and a half. Everyone on the team, without exception, received promotions.

Being successful is having others think you're successful. I think I have shown you enough now that if you don't believe it, you will at least watch for it and see how well it works.

The Corporate Politician's Image

To establish oneself in the world, one does all one can to seem established there already.

FRANÇOIS, DUC DE LA ROCHEFOUCAULD (1613–80)

Once, when I thought I should have received a promotion and didn't, I asked my boss why. The conversation went something like this:

Me: Why didn't I get that honcho job?

Boss: You still need a little more experience in your current position. (Notice the Master Corporate Politician answer—everyone can use more experience.)

Me: Do you really believe that?

Boss: Yes. (Master Corporate Politicians stick to their lies, even if it almost kills them.)

Me: You're lying to me, aren't you? Do you really feel that way?

Boss: Well, maybe not, but the big boss and I think the other guy was more qualified. (Notice how he brings in his boss to add authority to the decision.)

Me: You're shitting me! (A calculated risk on my part, confronting the boss.)

Boss: No lie. (He says it with a straight face, but I know him well enough to know he's lying.)

Me: How's he more qualified? I have more and better experience. I have a masters degree, and he has only an associate. (I was wasting my time, and I knew it—once a decision is made, management never changes its mind.)

Boss: There are other things besides education and experience. (Unusual for him to answer a question like that.)

Me: Such as?

Boss: My boss doesn't think you look professional enough. He doesn't think you dress like a professional, and your haircut looks like a blue-light special from K-Mart. (He was right! I had gambled on getting the promotion and was living way above my means. I was using every money-saving device I could think of, and clothes and haircuts were items that, at the time, I thought I could skimp on.)

Me: What about my ability to do the job? (I was sure this was just another one of his Master Corporate Politician answers designed to send me away, but it had a ring of possible truth.)

Boss: The selection of the other guy had nothing to do with ability. In fact, I think you're more competent than he is. (Was the boss being honest and candid for the first time in his life?) The selection was based on appearance because, as you know, that position has high visibility and will lead to another promotion in less than two years. You just don't look as if you can handle that higher position, and the other guy does.

Me: Why didn't you tell me? I would've changed.

Boss: Some things you just don't tell people.

After the frank discussion with my boss, I was mad. I was angry because management had rejected me because of my appearance, not my ability. I stayed mad for a week and even updated my resume. The next week, I observed the guy who had gotten the job. My boss was right; I had to admit it to myself. The guy looked as if he had just stepped out of the pages of *Esquire*—every hair was in place, his shirts were monogrammed, and the creases on his trousers were so sharp they could have cut steel.

I learned from that experience. From that day forward, I dressed as well as I could afford, and I had my hair done at a stylist's. I removed one more excuse from management for not promoting me.

Do you ever wonder what executives carry in their brief-cases when they walk into the office in the morning? A few of them don't carry anything, and a few carry only their lunch. You're kidding, you say? Believe me, not every executive works until seven at night and then carries more work home to do after supper. The briefcase, like a white shirt and tie, is standard equipment whether you need one or not—all hot shots carry one, and if you're a hot shot or want to be, you better have one.

In addition to briefcases, clothes are important for the perception of success. Books are a good example of what I'm talking about. You'll pick a book off the rack if it attracts your attention. If it's clad in a dull jacket and doesn't stand out, you'll pass it by unless you're specifically looking for it. You have to look as if you just walked out of the stockholders's meeting: that means expensive clothes and shoes, and lots of them. You can't get by with only a couple of expensive suits, because people notice what you're wearing and start to ask themselves, "Doesn't this guy have but one change of clothes?"

Haircuts should be done by a stylist, not by your spouse or friend. Remember, your appearance, like a book cover, is the first thing anyone sees. My wife is good with a pair of scissors—she cuts the children's hair, and occasionally she has trimmed mine. But the difference between her work and a stylist's is noticeable. Shine your shoes daily, and for God's sake, bathe daily and brush your teeth. The difference will pay off in the long run. It's all part of the image that says you're a honcho because, if nothing else, you look like one.

Women, you have a real problem. Notice that men have only half a dozen suits, and they wear them all the time. Okay for guys, right? They all do it, so it's okay. The women you are competing with, however, all seem to have family wealth or have married millionaires—where do they get the money for all those clothes? Some of them even change during the day. How do you compete with this? I studied my father's third wife, and she broke the code for me. She would buy expensive clothes in classic styles, but clothing to match the others in her wardrobe. A new jacket would go with several skirts or slacks she already owned, and she could wear it forever because it was a classic style. A new jacket means a new look— several new looks. My oldest daughter doesn't buy the classic styles, but modern. Since I am such a miser with the clothing budget, she is able to accomplish the same result by shopping bargains and buying nonname brands. She looks great all the time. Hair, clothes, shoes, and makeup are very important for your image. Not only do you have to look professional, but you have to look feminine and attractive, a burden not placed on men.

Being successful is looking successful.

Summary

Corporate politics is a game. It consists of knowing the right people, buttering them up, and becoming one of "their people." You should keep records of what happens in your professional life because those records may save you later. When you use the tactics in this book, be careful not to overuse them. Like food, too much of the same thing tends to diminish the appetite. Look and act as if you're somebody. If you look important, you will be.

chapter 2

The Art of
Jungle Warfare

This chapter deals with the other general rules and guidelines a successful Master Corporate Politician needs to survive. Although they are not the most important ones, an understanding of these additional rules and guidelines is necessary for survival. When you can look like a showhorse, work like a workhorse, tap dance your way out of any situation, remember a million jokes, play the got'cha game with the best of them, hire only winners, use foul language when you need to, and understand the meaning of a title, you're ready to move on to the more sophisticated applications of corporate politics.

Showhorses

Think of all the really successful men and women you know. Do you know a single one who didn't learn very young the trick of calling attention to himself in the right quarters?

STORM JAMESON (1891–1986)

People are like horses. There are many varieties of horses, but basically there are two main categories. The gubernatorial election in Georgia a few years ago pitted two competent men against one another. George Busby in his winning campaign used an expression to describe himself: *A Workhorse, Not a Showhorse*. The people of the great State of Georgia, like the senior management of most corporations, claimed they wanted a workhorse, but they really wanted a showhorse. Governor Busby, by using the slogan to proclaim himself a workhorse, was being a showhorse. Senior management likes to think they want workhorses, but they really want showhorses that can work. If they can't have that, they'll pick a straight showhorse every time because showhorses look as if they can work. Workhorses look like workhorses.

If you assume horses are of one category or the other, work or show, then you can draw a parallel to people—workers or politicians. However, since people are obviously more complex than horses and since the environment they must survive in is equally complex, you can assume that some people can do both. Some people do.

Which is preferable, you ask? The standard issue—Master Corporate Politician answer—is, "It depends." On what? It depends on your career aspirations. If you haven't heard that one, then you haven't talked to your boss about your career, you haven't worked in a large corporation. It's standard pabulum to pass out to ambitious employees. In this case, however, it is true. If you are, for example, an engineer, you enjoy being an engineer, and you don't have aspirations of being chief engineer, then you have no need to read further—you want to be a workhorse, and you should return this book to the shelf and get a novel. However, if you are being eaten up with ambition to be the chairman of the board, you need to be a showhorse. If you aren't, you will be disappointed when you reach middle age and realize you're a workhorse, doomed to middle management. Nobody said it was easy being a Master Corporate Politician.

Being a successful Master Corporate Politician is looking like a showhorse and working like a workhorse.

The Tap Dance

The best liar is he who makes the smallest amount of lying go the longest way.
SAMUEL BUTLER (1835–1902)

The most used tool of a Master Corporate Politician is his or her ability to tap dance. Tap dancing is improvisation. It's the art and practice of defending yourself to a hostile audience when you have, or appear to have, screwed up, and you don't have an acceptable answer. It's usually a defense mechanism that fends off wrath or postpones it until you're more prepared to handle it. It's also the clever art of mixing two or more Master Corporate Politician tactics together so no one can pin anything on you. Other names for tap dancing are:

- Winging it

- Bullshitting your way through

- Jiving

- Shuffling

- Fancy footwork

- Off the top of your head

- Ad-libbing

One of the goals of this book is to reveal some finer aspects of tap dancing and how to use them. I know very few senior corporate executives or politicians who are not expert tap dancers—they have to be to get to the top and to stay there.

How does one tap dance? Let me illustrate.

The Situation: (This month's production schedule is in jeopardy and you don't think you can pull it off. The boss expressed concern a week ago, and things have only gotten worse. You've hidden your real thoughts from everyone until you can find a good excuse to hang the failure on.)

The Boss: You're flat on your ass with this month's shipments. Last time we talked, you said things were going to improve. You should already have shipped six widgets.

You: (Ostensibly surprised and unprepared, but totally ready—you knew it was coming and have been preparing for it mentally.) Yes sir, I've had some problems, particularly with purchased parts, but we've turned them around, and my people believe the schedule can be made if we don't hit any more snags. (You throw some numbers and figures at him that he wouldn't know if they were right or not, and he leaves, convinced that you know what you're doing.)

This dialogue contains a mixture of what's called Lip of the cup, Number dazzle, Disassociation, Blame your employees, and Blame procurement. These tactics and others are covered in more detail later in the book. You told a white lie, and you set him up to accept another snag if you run into one (see Fireproofing, page 7). Your white lie gave you time to concoct a better story and determine whom you're going to blame for your failure to make this month's schedule. If you can't find anyone else, you've already set up your staff and purchasing to be blamed. If he asks you again before you're ready, tell him the same thing you just told him. It worked before, and if he was stupid enough to let you use that many tactics on him at the same time, he will again.

Learning to Tap Dance

Learning carries within itself certain dangers because out of necessity one has to learn from one's enemies.
LEON TROTSKY (1879–1940)

Prior to this book, one of the best ways to learn tap dancing was by selling used cars for a few years, by trial and error, or by observing the Master Corporate Politicians at work. Like most college-educated professionals, I didn't sell used cars—although I do recommend it—and it wasn't until I was well past thirty years old that I began to observe the masters with a keen, self-educating interest. The first ten years of my career were spent getting the stuffing kicked out of me, as the price paid for learning what, and what not, to say or do. I learned my lessons reasonably well, but as the engineers say, "I met spec for current loads, but I wasn't stressed for anything better."

What changed? I did. After two corporations and at least a half dozen jobs, I changed. I watched those men who were successful and saw how they tap danced. Every time I went to a meeting with my boss, or his boss, or someone senior to me, I listened to what they said, and particularly how they said it. I started dressing like them and emulating their every successful move. I became a senior-management clone. I wore the ugly wing-tip shoes and the conservative blue and black suits; I was soon accepted and considered part of "their crowd." Occasionally, one of my seniors would let me know what he was doing prior to doing it; I was able to watch the game as it unfolded and see how it was played.

If you get nothing else from this book, learn to note how your boss and other superiors handle tap dancing. If I knew all the answers, I would be the president of my own corporation, or of the United States, or the universe.

Attempting to categorize the various techniques is fun. Try it; you'll enjoy being a sociologist, even if every technique you observe isn't suited to your style.

The Got'cha Game

> *Hence that general is skillful in attack whose opponent does not know what to defend; and he is skillful in defense whose opponent does not know what to attack.*
> **SUN TZU** (6TH–5TH CENTURY B.C.)

Some managers love to play got'cha. If you're unfortunate enough to encounter one of them, it will give you a career-threatening opportunity to practice your tap dancing. The rules are as follows:

1. Find out something bad about another manager's department.

2. Guard this information carefully—don't talk to the responsible manager because if you do he'll be prepared to answer for it when you reveal it in step #3.

3. Reveal the got'cha at a general-manager-level or higher meeting. The result will give the general manager the impression that you're on top of things and the guy you're dropping the got'cha on is not.

4. Watch the accused manager tap dance or die.

   Examples of common got'chas are:

   Purchasing: A missed delivery promise on a critical part, or a critical vendor went bankrupt.

   Manufacturing: A last-minute scrap tag on a critical part.

   Engineering: Notice that a critical part can't be made, or won't fit into the assembly for which it was designed.

   Quality: Notice that a lot of parts that were accepted as good are now failing in final assembly.

   Accounting: A critical vendor has stopped shipments because his bills aren't being paid.

   Data processing: The usual—the programs don't work, or they never did.

   Sales: Salespeople do no wrong! Don't even try to got'cha a salesman. If you do, he'll just tap dance his way out of it. You lose!

Got'chas are fun to play on people you like and even more fun to do to guys you don't. I try to carry a got'cha on every one of my peers when I go before the general manager. I don't use them unless I have to, because as the man responsible for purchasing, I have always been vulnerable to attack. I don't recommend you practice this game unless you're secure enough in your position that you can stand retribution, because once you act, it will come.

 # Jokes

> *My way of joking is to tell the truth. It's the funniest joke in the world.*
>
> **GEORGE BERNARD SHAW** (1856–1950)

Attention and recognition of management above you is important. Just having them know your name will add points in your favor when promotions or salary reviews are held. One way of letting management know you is through jokes. Everybody loves to be entertained, and everybody loves a clown.

To illustrate, let me tell you how an obscure practical joker got recognition that allowed him to rise to middle management. The big boss had a large nose and wore heavy, dark-rimmed glasses. The joker bought everyone in the department a pair of those novelty glasses with the large nose and moustache, cut off the moustache, and had everyone wear them. We all looked like the boss. The joke succeeded in getting the joker recognition, and he was promoted.

Another joker took the boss's picture from several copies of the company newspaper and inserted them under the middle piece of the rotary dial in our phones and the big boss's phone. The big boss thought it was funny, and both the joker and the boss got recognition.

In addition to practical jokes, funny people have a way of attracting attention. A guy who can remember jokes and keep his friends laughing will form few enemies and will rise in an organization because of it. The only danger of telling jokes and being everyone's friend is that you may attract the reputation of being a clown and therefore of not being capable of anything but being a clown.

I would recommend you try to remember jokes. They can hide a void in your personality, particularly if you're like me—not very good at small talk. Practical jokes, when used with discretion, are good tools to show affection and respect.

Hiring Smart

A man is known by the company he organizes.
AMBROSE BIERCE (1842–1914)

As an accountant, early in my career I worked with a chemist who had risen to production manager. He was a workhorse and a technician. He didn't play games and he didn't kiss ass, but he was successful because of his hiring techniques. He believed in hiring the best employees that money could buy, overpaying them, and if they didn't meet spec, firing them. Using this strategy, he was able to collect the most competent individuals in the industry and keep them. He paid them more money than they could make anywhere else in the country, and they worked with people who were just as competent as they were. He was a winner. So was his organization and the company.

The application is simple. Hire people who are more competent than you are, keep them well paid, and they'll push you to the top. A lot of managers consider this a threat and avoid hiring someone who might outshine them in the eyes of the top management. This thinking is what's wrong with a lot of organizations today—they have no depth. It's irrational organizationally because if the manager dies, there's no ready heir apparent and the company will be forced to replace him or her with a substandard individual or hire from the outside. It's not wise for you as an individual because if you're the only one in the organization capable of doing your job, you're limited because you're not replaceable—they can't promote you if they don't have someone who can take your place.

Hiring people who are as good or better than you are is wise both for you and your organization.

 # Language

> 'Twas but my tongue, 'twas not my soul that swore.
> **EURIPIDES** (480–406 B.C.)

First, I must say that using foul language is generally not a good idea, but I use it all the time. I use it because the three years I spent in the Army taught me a whole new vocabulary and I became, unfortunately, very comfortable with it. There's a time and a place to use a military vocabulary, and there are some definite times and places not to use it.

Let me begin by defining the organizational levels where it can be used, and then the situations. Subordinates will accept just about any language you use—*they don't have any choice.*

They'll talk behind your back and call you foulmouthed, but so what? Women subordinates sometimes object to foul language, but most modern women have heard it before and won't make waves to force you to stop. In some weird way, men accept foul language as a sign of manhood—real men use it and wimps don't.

Peers will generally accept any form of language you use. If they have a strong dislike of foul language, you may find that any relationship you have with them will suffer. My suggestion is not to use it with people who don't, and to use it with people who do. In mixed company, don't; and when you find yourself with a mixture of people who do and don't, don't.

Dealing with superiors requires caution. I've seen some very competent individuals whose careers have slowed and halted due to their inappropriate use of foul language. They were labeled as foulmouthed louts—unpolished people that need to be kept hidden away—and regardless of their accomplishments, management wouldn't give them further consideration. I generally respond to superiors in the same fashion as I do to peers. If a superior is a man and uses foul language, he does so for a reason. It is usually the macho image referred to here. His rating of his male subordinates may be based on his perception of their masculinity. When dealing with levels above your boss, use foul language only in emergencies.

There is but one situation, in my opinion, where foul language will be tolerated in almost every case—an emergency. Emergencies cannot be defined by me because everybody has his or her own definition, and, depending on the situation, anything could be an emergency. I used the word "bastard" to describe the vice president of logistics to my vice president when I was just a first-line supervisor. The other vice president had pulled a got'cha on my vice president and I needed him to respond quickly to the situation. He laughed—it broke the tension—and I got his help. It showed him I cared about his career and was a member of his team. With another company, I used the term "sons' a 'bitches" with my boss's boss, a vice president, to describe the Accounts Payable Department when they became so backlogged in paying our bills that several of my suppliers had put our Fortune 100 company on credit hold. I got his attention.

If they have never heard you use foul language, and then you use it, it's a signal that something is very wrong, and they will generally listen to you. Use it sparingly, and it'll become an effective tool.

The use of foul language to punctuate pertinent points has also been effective for me. I use the *F* word as the foremost adjective. Using this word adds emphasis if it isn't overused. A statement such as, "no f—ing way," is much more final than just, "no way." To insult someone, "you're out of your f—ing mind," is more insulting than to say, "you're out of your mind."

The *S* word seems to add flavor and punch to my sentences. Which conveys the most intensity? "I'm not going to put up with this shit anymore," or "I'm not going to tolerate this anymore." I'm sure you've heard these, and more, but here's the message: If you use foul language, use it sparingly and for effect. Don't get into the habit of some people, whose foul language has become part of their personality.

Curse words never bother me; bad taste does. Two examples of bad taste are talking about sexual experiences in mixed company or talking about another employee's weaknesses to that employee's peer. I'm not attempting to moralize—do whatever you want—but if you want to reach the top, be careful about what you talk about, and to whom. When I hear a man talk about sexual experiences, even in strictly male company, I wonder why he's doing it. Is he trying to persuade the other men that he's as masculine as they are? Is he trying to get them to envy him? I don't understand it; neither do most men or women. Talking about subordinates to other subordinates scares me. When my boss talks to me about one of my peers, I wonder whether he is talking about me to one of my peers. Your people will feel the same. This principle also holds true with peer relations. Don't discuss one peer's performance with another peer. He won't trust you, and he may even tell the other person what you said about her. You will have made an enemy.

Be cautious in what you say, whom you say it to, and how you say it.

What's in a Title?

Authority is not a quality one person "has," in the sense that he has property or physical qualities. Authority refers to an interpersonal relation in which one person looks upon another as somebody superior to him.

ERICH FROMM (1900–1980)

What's in a title? Nothing, unless you don't have one. I remember when I was just starting out it seemed to me that the guys with the fancy titles really had power. I thought if I ever made it to manager, I would be king of the world. Guess what? Being a manager or a director isn't much different from what you are before except the problems are tougher. You might make more money, but you *earn* more money.

EAT—OR BE EATEN

Do titles scare you? Should they? They used to frighten me a little. When I was a first-line supervisor and was called into the vice president's office, my knees were knocking and the adrenalin was pumping. This guy could grind me any time he wanted, and nobody was going to stop him. The higher I rose in the world of corporate politics, the more I realized that the guys with the titles were real people just like me, and they couldn't do anything to me unless I let them. Guys at the top are regular guys; they do things just like you and me. They have feelings, get their asses chewed, have trouble making decisions, and don't like things rocking the boat. They're human, and you can talk to them.

Another thing about titles—you don't know what they mean. Have you ever tried to hire anyone? All your applicants were managers or directors of something. When you inquire about their staff size and responsibility, you find they were first-line supervisors with limited responsibility and no authority. You don't hit the big leagues until you're managing over fifty people and have at least two levels below you. When a person is managing supervisors of supervisors, he or she is in the big leagues.

Look at your local supermarket. They have a produce manager, dry-goods manager, bakery manager, and so on. What are they managing? Putting food out on shelves. Look at your local restaurant. They have managers for the kitchen, bar, waitresses. Small companies must have managers, and they do, but are they managers of the same magnitude as those in large corporations? They may be managers, but they don't have the same responsibility, authority, or staff of a Master Corporate Politician.

Don't let titles bother you. They don't mean anything.

30

Summary

I hope by now that you are getting a feel for what life in the corporate world is really all about. There are many unwritten rules and guidelines that you will need to understand to survive and thrive. Looking professional, tap dancing, knowing the games that are played, using humor, hiring good people, using language appropriately, and understanding titles are but a few of the things you must master to rise to the top of the organization chart. This chapter and the preceding one served as an introduction and foundation for what is to follow. Remember that corporate politics is a game, and if you lose, they'll grind you up. This book is designed to prevent you from winding up as the main course on some fat Master Corporate Politician's dining table.

chapter 3

Stalking Your Prey

One trait of Master Corporate Politicians is that things seem "just to go their way." Is it luck, or is skill involved? You better believe there's no luck in getting your way—it takes work and skill. This chapter is dedicated to showing you some of the tactics the big boys use to get things going their way. I have intentionally left out the tactic of simply asking—you know it already. The Master Corporate Politician rarely asks—it's just not done. That would keep him or her from playing their games and using their tactics.

Master Corporate Politicians go to the manager who will agree with what they want and avoid the manager who will disagree with them. They occasionally just say "no!" to see what happens. They scream, they get angry, and they negotiate, but they always win. They remove their adversaries, are patient and methodical in their designs, and they follow instructions regardless of how stupid. They use many tactics simultaneously and when all else fails, they threaten to quit.

This chapter will show you how they do it and will allow you to recognize these tactics and be prepared to combat them if necessary.

The Auction

*The general fact is that the most effective way of uti-
lizing human energy is through an organized rivalry,
which by specialization and social control is, at the
same time, organized co-operation.*

CHARLES HORTON COOLEY (1864–1929)

A corporate position that has grown over the past few years
is the matrix position mentioned earlier in which an
employee reports to two or more bosses. It would seem
tough, working for two or more people. In reality, it's much
simpler than working for just one. By working for two or
more people, you can divide and conquer or, in effect, get
what you want. If one boss doesn't like something, get the
other boss to like it. The resulting conflict will give you a 50
percent chance of getting what you want, and that is a higher average than the guy who works for only one boss. If one
of your bosses is an idiot, you can rely on the other one,
you'll hope, to add some sanity to your life.

I have been in a matrix position three times in my
career. I hated it at first, but, in time, when I learned the
ropes, I grew to love it. First, you normally don't have anyone working for you; I love the power, but I hate the problems associated with managing people. As a matrix manager, I could go and do whatever I wanted. I was in a position,
as one of the functional guys put it, of "dropping off turds
and leaving." They had to fix the problems; all I had to do
was identify them and chew the functional guys out because
they hadn't already found and fixed them. It was a wonder-
ful life.

How do you use a matrix position to get what you want? To begin with, matrix positions are only stepping stones to real power, a functional position. Usually, when you report to two or more bosses, they have some clout. You represent one of them to the other, and the goodwill between the two of them is what makes the system work. By exploiting the need for goodwill, you can come out ahead. They don't want conflict, either of them; they want things to run smoothly and without problems. If there are problems, they get angry with each other and it's up to you to patch things up. Both of them will be grateful.

Once you have been in the position for a few months, you will sense which of your bosses has the most power. Get on his or her good side. If a conflict arises between your bosses, claim that you're merely a messenger and cite the adage about not killing the messenger. Most people who work in matrix organizations understand your position, and you won't be sent to the grinder.

Use the bosses to get what you want. If you have trouble with one functional area, the one you want to head, tell the nonfunctional boss of your problems; subtly let him know of your qualifications for the position. Keep those qualifications in front of him at all times, but be subtle. Then let a functional manager know of your problems with his or her subordinate; also let him or her know of your qualifications and desire to hold the position—subtly.

You can use a matrix position to get the functional position you want if you're patient and careful. It can take years off your climb to the top. Seek out matrix positions and grab them when they're available, but be aware that you're vulnerable—both bosses will blame you and flip a coin to see whose grinder you get to die in if you are a failure. You don't want to be queued up to die in both boss's grinders.

Just Say "No!"

It is kindness to refuse immediately what you intend to deny.

PUBLILIUS SYRUS (1ST CENTURY B.C.)

Have you ever had the urge to just say no and see what happens? Try it. I took over a materials organization a few years ago, and the financial people had that organization creating mountains of paperwork to justify each expenditure. I told my staff to stop preparing it or sending it out. When the controller called to ask why I did that, I told him I just wasn't going to do it anymore. He said I would hear more on the matter, but I never did. I was able to put two people to other, more constructive work.

When the telephone solicitors call me at my home, I say no. I don't care what they're selling, I say no. When the budget control people wanted me to sign all purchase requisitions over a certain dollar amount, I said no and instructed my buyers to ignore their requirements. The problem went away.

The message of this section is to convey to you the knowledge that it's okay to say no. You can always recant and do what they want, but you might be lucky, like me, and get away with it. If not, refer to the next chapter and stall them to the point where it's no longer worth fighting for. A committee will kill anything.

The Screamers and How to Fight Them

*Nothing gives a fearful man more courage than
another's fear.*

UMBERTO ECO (b. 1932)

Somewhere back in the days of the caveman, leaders were taught that to be effective they had to scream at their people. It must have something to do with why dogs growl at each other and cats hiss at each other. Why do managers feel the need to scream? I don't know. Some of them just do.

What do you do when one of them screams at you? You can do two things. You can curl up your tail between your legs like most others, or you can bare your fangs and let the idiot know that you don't push around easily. I've always operated on the latter premise, and it has yet to hurt me. I watch my peers shiver and shake when the general manager roars and feel nothing but disgust. I understand that some people feel the need to roar, but it doesn't do a thing for me but make me angry. When the screaming is directed at me, I scream back with the same ferocity as the blasts that are directed at me. Sometimes it gets bloody, but I've never been punished for this form of behavior. It takes guts but, with most managers, it says you have backbone and are willing to fight it out if you have to. When you do it, however, always do it with respect and courtesy.

In those instances where you've clearly screwed up and are getting your just desserts, take what's coming to you. Remember, verbal abuse for the sake of abuse is cause for anger, and you need to control your response.

37

Effective Use of Anger

We praise a man who feels angry on the right grounds and against the right persons and also in the right manner at the right moment and for the right length of time.

ARISTOTLE (384–322 B.C.)

A corollary to the preceding section is the use of anger, both real and pretend. Most people don't like fights. It would be great if everybody always got along but, unfortunately, they don't. When someone gets angry, the natural tendency is to pacify him and get him to settle down. Pacify is another word for "give in." This knowledge can be very useful to a Master Corporate Politician. *Don't be afraid to get angry to get your way!*

What is pretend anger? It is anger that's not real, but appears to be real to help you get your way. A good example of pretend anger occurred a few years ago. I was attending a meeting with my former boss, then a director. He exploded, his anger falling on the individual who was refusing to cooperate with him.

The boss's face turned red, and I imagine that the hair stood up on the back of his neck. His mouth spurted every sort of foul language I had ever heard and I almost imagined steam snorting from his nostrils. His anger was frightening to me and to everyone else in the room. Using this tactic, my boss got a small concession and ultimately used it as a wedge to get what he wanted. After the meeting, when we were alone, I asked him what had made him so angry. He smiled at me and told me he wasn't mad and never had been. I shook my head in disbelief—I knew anger when I saw it. "It's true," he said. "I never lose my temper when I'm dealing with those

might give you the inflated salary, but don't count on it. More likely, he'll negotiate with you and give you a figure much closer to the one you had in mind. If you quote a realistic number up front, he'll give you an offer at that salary, or less. I do it all the time. I always cut a guy's salary demand a little when making an offer.

Our contracts department made a mistake and signed us up for a job we couldn't do for the money we were going to receive. They had grossly underestimated the personnel necessary to do the job, leaving me short of budget. While trying to figure out how I was going to squeeze the effort of one additional person out of an already overworked staff, another program manager asked me how long it would take to get his fully funded program material purchased. I knew that with existing staff, I would have it done in about two months, but told him I needed six—he had budget, and I needed it. He screamed that my answer wasn't acceptable and that I had to do it in less than three. I told him that with the meager staff I had, and by working overtime, I might be able to squeeze it down to five months. He asked how many additional people it would take to get it down to the three he wanted. I was reasonable and told him two more people would be needed to meet his impossible deadline. He screamed about that, and after several hours of negotiations, we agreed that if I got one more person and worked overtime, I would do it in three months. I got an extra person, paid for by him, to work on the underfunded job. We both got what we wanted.

Asking for more than you need is one of the tactics used by Master Corporate Politicians to get what they want. You should remember this tactic and use it in every application possible. It will help you get what you want.

Removing an Adversary Kindly

The only way to win is to fight on the side of your adversaries.

FRANCIS PICABIA (1878–1953)

Let me define what I mean by adversary. Anyone who stands in the way of what you want is an adversary. She could be your best friend, but if she holds a job you want, she's an adversary. If you have a problem employee, she's an adversary. What's the best way to remove an adversary and have him or her want to be removed? Find the adversary a better job.

I've used this tactic only a few times. Normally if the person's an idiot, everybody knows it. Removing a boss is the toughest because if he's worthless, everyone knows it and you're just stuck with him. I once wanted a position held by a man who was more polished than I was. He wasn't any smarter, but he knew tap dancing and a few other tricks I hadn't yet mastered. I was told by a friend of mine in graduate school of an opening in his company. The opening was for an individual who met the qualifications held by both me and Mister Shoe Polish. I told Mister Polish, he applied, and got the job. I was promoted into his job.

Getting rid of dud employees is also tough. Through counseling, I inform them that their performance is substandard. Usually this is enough to start them on the trail of finding another job. Finding them a job is tough because you can't tell them you want them to leave. If you do, they will give you less than they are already giving, until they find another job.

As the senior manager of a large materials organization, I get calls all the time from headhunters, or private personnel recruiters—they're either trying to place me in a position they have or are trying to place an individual they have in my organization. I pass on the names of troubled employees to these people. Usually, either the counseling sessions, employee efforts at finding an organization appreciating his or her limited skills, or my efforts through the headhunters, works. If you want to be a successful Master Corporate Politician, learn to get rid of employees that don't meet spec and won't improve. This is so important that I go into over thirty different ways to do this later in the book. Managing subordinates is the second most important thing in a Master Corporate Politician's life, and yours. If you forgot what is most important, reread Rule 1 on page 2.

Eat the Elephant One Bite at a Time

I am extraordinarily patient provided I get my own way in the end.

MARGARET THATCHER (b. 1925)

There is an old saying, "The only way to eat an elephant is one bite at a time." Getting what you want may mean fighting to get only a portion of what you want and then expanding it to where it covers what your objective is. Often, if you try to take the whole objective in one battle, you'll lose. Wise generals know this and that's why it takes them years to win a war. Why did it take Grant over a year to push Lee out of Petersburg? It took him a year because if he had tried to win the battle in a single fight, he would have lost.

Here is a corporate example. I was in a matrix position—you'll move in and out of them many times in your career if you're smart—and the functional boss wouldn't help me do the job I was assigned. He wanted to keep all the power, but wouldn't do the job. What could I do? I could have complained to the program people I supported, but that would have destroyed my relationship with my functional boss. Instead, I talked the program people into taking over a small portion of the task. The program took over a portion of production control—a critical area that was causing my functional boss a great deal of embarrassment. They put me in charge of running it and left all other tasks with my functional boss. I cleaned up the problems in production control and moved to another area. Soon, I owned all functional areas that supported me. Did I do this by design? You bet!

Another example occurred when I watched my boss, a functional manager, work his way to vice president. He ran material operations, a large group consisting of over four hundred people; the group determined the requirements for production material and provided warehousing for six factories. He needed some procurement experience if he wished to make vice president. How did he do it? He started by convincing the vice president of manufacturing that there would be a considerable head-count reduction if he allowed the merger of production control into his organization. He got it, and reduced redundancy and head count by 20 percent. Second, he convinced the vice president of material he could do a better job of vendor follow-up than the director of procurement could. Since he now owned production control, he was able to do this by blaming all factory problems on procurement. He took over vendor follow-up, and all problems with that organization seemed to vanish. He then took over general procurement, and now he owns it all. If he had gone in to the general manager and suggested his ultimate organization, he would have created enemies of the vice presidents of materials and production. He ate the elephant one bite at a time, and he did it by design because we talked about his strategy as he implemented it.

Am I suggesting you don't propose organization changes that favor your career? Absolutely not. Do it cautiously, but always let the boss know what you think would make a smoother-running organization. Keep your ideas couched in terms of helping him or her do a better job of running their organization. If you're a performer and know what you're doing, he or she will remember what you said and may actually implement it without too much arm-twisting on your part.

Remember, that your journey to the top will involve designs, and you must plan them strategically to eat the elephant one bite at a time. Only the boa constrictor can eat its whole prey in one bite, and even a boa wouldn't tackle something so large. Getting what you want means inching your way along, bit by bit.

Patience Wins

Perhaps there is only one cardinal sin: impatience.
Because of impatience we were driven out of Paradise,
because of impatience we cannot return.

W. H. AUDEN (1907–73)

This section is similar to the previous one except it has a different theme. Most young people I meet today want to be chairman of the board before they're thirty and will settle for it before they reach forty. Fat chance! Business is like a pyramid, with the young on the bottom and the old and wise on the top. Notice that I said wise, because the just plain old are either on the bottom or in the middle, not on top. So how does one get there?

One thing all the big shots have that most young managers don't, is patience. What do I mean by patience? I mean the willingness to wait for what you want. If your plan is right and you have the right stuff, it will eventually work. You can always jump ship and find another job, which I recommend occasionally if you're in a hurry; but if you like the company you're with and don't want to leave, then you must be patient and let your plans hatch.

Allow me to tell you about some of my successes with patience. I was the functional manager, and an ambitious matrix manager kept trying to take over areas that belonged to me. He was using several tactics in this book and was very good at it. I was near my rope's end when I sat down and prepared a plan to get rid of him. I instructed my staff to ignore him, stop sending him memos, and stop telling him what was happening. They did, and he became ineffective. He became angry with me and my people, but we continued to shut him out. In time, he found another job because he felt useless in the matrix position. It worked because I had the patience to wait almost a year for him to get fed up with his job and seek another. By the way, I also helped him find the other job.

If you have a problem, prepare a plan to fix it. The plan may take a year or so, but put it together and wait. If the plan is any good, it will work, and you will have solved your problem.

Just As He Told You

Reasonable orders are easy enough to obey; it is capricious, bureaucratic or plain idiotic demands that form the habit of discipline.

BARBARA TUCHMAN (1912–89)

Got an idiot for a boss? Got a boss you hate? The best way to get rid of these guys is to do precisely what they say. Everybody makes mistakes, and if you don't question or argue, then the fault of the mistake will fall on the person who told you to do what caused it.

This tactic is particularly effective when you have a boss who doesn't know what's going on. There are a lot of them out there, and if you have one, this tactic is for you. An example of how an employee of mine used this tactic on me occurred when I told him to clean up his office—it was a pigpen. He did exactly what I told him to do. He threw away valuable files and documents, but he did clean up the office. When I asked for the files, he told me that I instructed him to throw away all that stuff, and he did. I wanted to fire him, but he did exactly what I told him to do. Needless to say, he didn't progress any more in my organization.

Does the tactic work? It works if your boss is screwing up all the time. If he or she screws up only occasionally, it can get you run across the slicing machine a few times or terminally placed (no more promotions).

I used this tactic effectively when I was right out of college. My boss was an imbecile and arrogant to boot. I hated him and wished I had chosen another major. I learned this tactic almost by accident because this first boss was the kind of guy that insisted you do it exactly as he told you—no argument, no discussion. He told me to clean up some general-ledger accounts using a unique program that ignored the basics of double-entry bookkeeping. The program was designed to clean up the odd cents that were left in accounts where it was more cost effective to just write it off than to research the reason. I was told to write off thousands of dollars, and I did. The controller found out about my actions and was going to reprimand me for it before I told him my boss had told me to do it that way. He understood, and that day my boss was terminated.

Does it work? You bet! Be careful in its application though because when one of the boss's directions backfires, he's a Master Corporate Politician and will use every trick in this book to crucify you. He can do it only if he doesn't screw up all the time, however; if he screws up regularly, he may turn you into meat when you follow his directions. A vice president was once chewing me out for doing something and I responded that I had done only what he had requested. He said, "Yes, I told you to do it, but I didn't tell you to do something stupid."

Soften Him Up

> Sure I am of this, that you have only to endure to conquer. You have only to persevere to save yourselves.
> **SIR WINSTON CHURCHILL** (1874–1965)

Most of you have never seen a combat assault. Normally, the artillery bombards the area with high explosives, then jets come in with bombs and napalm, and then helicopter gunships rake the area with machine guns and rockets. The military calls it softening up the area. The same philosophy applies to corporate politics.

When you want something, start by softening up your boss or your boss's boss. I wanted pay raises for all my staff. It was unheard of in the company I worked for. I went to the vice president and told him I was having trouble hiring people because when I did, I had to hire them in at higher salaries than my existing staff. My supervisors were getting angry that I was having to hire people making more money than they were. The vice president understood my problem, but offered no solution. Within a month, another one of my people quit and I went to the vice president again and told him that unless I did something with the salaries in my department, I was going to lose all my people. He nodded his understanding, but offered no help. When another one left, I went in again. This time when I asked, I got a raise for all my people.

The message here is that if the Master Corporate Politician hears something often enough, he begins to believe it's the truth. To use this tactic, keep the story that you want the Master Corporate Politician to believe always in front of him. If he sees it often enough, he might accept it as a fact, and you might be able to achieve what you want.

Threaten to Quit

Defeat doesn't finish a man—quit does. A man is not finished when he's defeated. He's finished when he quits.
RICHARD M. NIXON (1913–94)

I've never used this tactic, but I've seen it used quite effectively by many Master Corporate Politicians. To understand this tactic, let me tell you how some positions are filled in the higher ranks of a corporation. Many of the positions are filled by friends of the boss's boss, or higher. Somewhat like the kingdoms of olden days, the princes, counts, and barons aren't necessarily related to the king. The king spent more time fighting with these guys than he did with his country's enemies. It's the same in corporate politics.

When you know you are "wired" to the top, you can push your boss around by threatening to quit if you don't get your way. The message that comes across is like when one child says to another, "I'm going to tell my momma." By threatening to quit, the astute Master Corporate Politician knows that his patron will want to know why and will talk him out of it by promising to fix the guy that won't get on with the program.

Having this tactic used on you can be frightening. What do you say? You wish you were Dirty Harry holding a 44 magnum in front of his face and could say, "Go ahead, Punk. Make my day." You can't say that, so it immediately puts you on the defensive. What do you do or say that will allow you to maintain the superior position? I don't know. That's one of the reasons this is such a good tactic.

Allow me to share a few examples of how I've seen this tactic work. I was the production control manager of an electronics product line. The general manager hired a man named Bill, one of his church buddies, to run production control on the nonelectronics product line. Right after he took the job, Bill wanted to make radical changes in our systems and procedures. He didn't know what he was doing, and his changes were going to screw up my smooth-running operation. He went to our director and requested the changes. The director called me in and we discussed them. I closed my arguments by saying that the changes were the stupidest thing I had ever heard. The general manager's buddy responded that if he couldn't have the tools he needed to do his job, then he didn't want to work here any more. I laughed out loud, but the director and I both knew he had been threatened. We compromised, and some changes were made.

The man used the same tactic again less than two weeks later on another subject, and again the following week. This time, I said, "Oh, no. Poor Old Bill's going to quit again," and my director laughed. Bill had broken one of the foremost rules of corporate politics—he had overused a tactic. Bill didn't last long after that. The director went out of his way to run him off.

Sometimes you can use a combination of tactics to respond to the quitting threat. The vice president decided to create matrix positions reporting to him, not to me, to help me control my major subcontracts. The positions were filled with political appointees who didn't know anything about subcontract management and soon became a real irritant to me. Not only did they take up enormous amounts of time from me and my staff, but they were giving my suppliers bad directions that conflicted with my contracts. I had to shut them down, and I did it by cutting off the flow of information to them. What they didn't know about, they couldn't get involved in.

One of the matrix guys, the only one with an IQ close to the wattage in a light bulb and an appointee of the general manager, figured out what I was doing and went to my vice president. The matrix guy said I wasn't cooperating and that he couldn't do his job.

My vice president listened politely and promised to look into it. He stalled and hoped the problem would go away. Light Bulb was persistent and brought it up again and again and again. He finally threatened to quit. When he did, I was directed to cooperate with him. What did I do? I smiled and said, "Yes, sir," and didn't do a damn thing. Another threat to quit and another session with my vice president. More of the same. Light Bulb did get some changes from me, but he had to go to the general manager to get them. Three months later I found Light Bulb another job, and my problems went away.

This tactic is effective in getting what you want. To use it, you need to be secure in your job, and it's much more effective if you use it in combination with other tactics. If it's the only tactic you have, you'll wear it out, and then you won't have any.

Summary

Getting your way is only one of the many tools you'll need to become a successful Master Corporate Politician. Life, like corporate politics, is a series of getting or not getting your way. It's hoped that after you have read this section you have learned a few tactics that will enable you to achieve the goal of getting your way. To this end, you have seen how a Master Corporate Politician will select the appropriate boss to get his or her way and the impact of just saying no! You now know about screaming, anger, and negotiation basics. You've read about how the Master Corporate Politician removes adversaries, is patient and methodical, and how he or she gets rid of an idiot boss. You've seen the use of multiple tactics and a method the Master Corporate Politician uses to leverage his or her worth by threatening to quit. By now, you know that these guys will do anything to get their way.

chapter 4

Strategies for the Hunt

Getting your way is as much about stalling the other guy's way as it is pushing your own. Competition for decision making is keen, even at the lowest levels of an organization. There are several methods of getting your way, and they should be used carefully, depending upon the situation. Like all tactics in this book, overuse tends to diminish effectiveness.

Most people rarely follow up on others. They are normally just too busy to do it, and they rely on the integrity of others to do what they say they'll do. The Master Corporate Politician uses this knowledge to his or her advantage when he or she wants to stall having to make a decision or give an answer. If you learn nothing else from this book, set up a method of follow-up where no one can stall you. I use a running-action item list. It is currently thirteen typewritten pages of answers and actions that I assigned to or requested from my staff and peers. At least once a week, I work it and update it with responses. It makes an individual look like a fool when you go to his boss with an action that needs working and you have six to eight weeks worth of the individual's excuses written down with the dates he gave them to you. It works.

The following pages list the stalling tactics used by some of the most successful politicians and some of the ways I use to combat them. How many times has a person said, "I'll get back to you," and hasn't? You've seen hundreds of good ideas get sent to a committee where they die of old age. You've witnessed Master Corporate Politicians tell you they would do it, and then they didn't. You've seen them make a federal case out of a minor problem, and you've seen them divert the attention away from their inaction or incompetence. You have to recognize what they're doing before you can combat them; and knowing these tactics will allow you to become much more effective at getting what you want.

I'll Get Back to You

> *There is no avoiding war; it can only be postponed to the advantage of others.*
> **NICCOLÒ MACHIAVELLI** (1469–1527)

Just saying, "I'll have to get back to you on that," gives you time to consider your next move, which could be no move. Wait until you're asked again and say the same thing, only add a feeble excuse as to why you haven't already gotten back to him. By stalling a decision or answer, you give yourself time to implement your own ideas or desires and you stall an opponent from implementing his ideas.

When presented with this tactic, I respond with, "When?" The next answer the Master Corporate Politician gives is usually, "I don't know. Let me look at it and I'll call you." To that I respond, "How much time do you think it'll take to look at it?"

The good Master Corporate Politician will answer in vague terms of a few days, a few weeks, or he's not sure. You have to pin him down as to when, or he's stalled you and you've lost. Get an exact time as to when you'll get your answer or decision.

Most people will accept the statement, "I'll get back to you." If that doesn't stop them, the promise, "I'll call you," seems to work. If you run into an eager beaver like me who pins you down to a specific date, when that date comes, call him and give him a new date. You can normally postpone it until the individual gives up interest, or until you're ready to confront whatever it is the eager beaver wants a decision or answer on. When this tactic is used on you, remind the individual that is stalling you of all previous promises and the urgency of your need for an answer/decision.

Let's Get Together and Talk About It

Life, as it is called, is for most of us one long postponement.

HENRY MILLER (1891–1980)

When you finally get pinned down and have to give a decision, you have another avenue for additional stalling. You can appease the person by saying, "Let's get together and talk about it. We need to discuss the issues." The eager beaver will respond with "When?" and you pick a date and time as far in the future as you think she'll accept. When that date and time comes, don't show up. Send a subordinate who doesn't have the power to make the decision—claim a meeting conflict.

You can use this tactic two to three times before the person seeking a decision starts to work her way up the organization chain seeking an answer.

When it gets to your superior, claim you tried to get together with the individual, but on those occasions when you tried, you had meeting conflicts. Claim to be angry that it got to his level and in the future, your boss should let you handle such minor details. Promise to get together with the individual as soon as possible. The boss generally will agree with such a recommendation because, after all, he's busy and too important to be involved with such trivia. Call the eager beaver and set up another meeting, proceeding as before. You can do it a couple more times.

How do you combat this? When the person you're trying to get a decision or an answer from misses your first meeting, schedule a meeting with his boss. Tell the boss that the decision is of such importance that it requires his personal attention—lie if you have to. Tell him you tried to meet with his subordinate for advice on how to approach him with the problem, but the poor man is so busy he hasn't been able to get together with you. Show him your log of conversations with the subordinate and tell him the decision or answer can't wait any longer. You'll get action, or if the boss starts to stall you, go up one more level. Keep going up until you find someone in the organization who'll give you what you need.

The only exception to the previous advice is if you're trying to get your own boss to answer you. In those cases, you can't jump the chain of command because your boss will consider you a disloyal employee and get his or her revenge. With a boss, all you can do is become such a polite pest that he or she finally answers you to make you go away.

Let's Put a Committee Together

A committee is an animal with four back legs.
JOHN LE CARRÉ (b. 1931)

When you get forced by your boss into tackling the decision or answer, the best way to stall further is to set up a committee. You can come up with a million reasons why a committee needs to look at a particular problem. A few examples:

- More than one functional area affected

- Requires the expertise of several people

- The experts need to look at it

- The implications of the decision could/will affect the profit picture for the coming year

Committees are death to the decision making process because they take forever to make a decision and whatever they come up with can be disputed. Try not to have yourself placed on the committee because you'll have difficulty distancing yourself from its recommendations. If at all possible place a loyal member of your staff on the committee with instructions to stall any consensus. Give him or her instructions to see to it that the committee covers all bases before making a decision. You want the committee to discuss everything *but* what you want discussed.

When the committee comes in with a recommendation, find fault with some portion of it and send the members back to do more work. You can keep the committee going indefinitely or until they disband due to a lack of interest.

If you're the eager beaver, you're in trouble. The guy you were forcing to make a decision has stalled you for an indefinite time. All you can hope to do is force the committee to make a recommendation quickly.

Normally what happens on committees is they're initially staffed with the people who know what they're doing, but over time the good people are replaced with those who don't have a clue. Good people don't like to waste time being part of stalling tactics or committees. They get themselves replaced. Also, good people are hard to find—they're critically needed—and their managers will pull them off the committees when the politics are right.

If a decision is needed and has been referred to a committee, the odds of getting a decision have fallen to where it may not be wise to continue championing the cause. Drop it. Let the committee and the big boys have it. If the problem that required the decision is not solved, bring it up again at a later date and start the whole process over again; and hope that this time the decision gets made before someone punts it off to a committee to die.

 ## Agree and Do What You Want

Of course I lie to people. But I lie altruistically—for our mutual good. The lie is the basic building block of good manners. That may seem mildly shocking to a moralist—but then what isn't?

QUENTIN CRISP (1908—1999)

Another method of stalling is to agree. Become the friendliest, most cooperative individual in the world. Whatever they want, they get—all smiles and agreement. The way you stall is by not doing anything. You agree to do whatever they want done, and then you do what you want. By the time they find out you haven't done anything and you run them through the "I'll get back to you," and the "let's get together," again, you've gained at least another month or two. When you get pinned down to go do what you've already agreed to do, confess you've had second thoughts and you need to study it some more—try to keep the cycle going as long as possible. Then, of course, you need a committee to look at it in more depth.

If you're all smiles and agreement, you may be able to use this tactic with regularity. If you lack the smooth, all smiles approach, you can use this tactic only once or twice in a career. It works, but you need to take great pains to make sure it doesn't ruin your credibility.

If your credibility is lessened, your ability to use any of the other stalling tactics is diminished. Even the stupidest Master Corporate Politician will know that you're no longer a person of your word.

Big Issue, Small Problem

I have yet to see any problem, however complicated, which, when you looked at it in the right way, did not become still more complicated.

POUL ANDERSON (b. 1926)

Another delaying tactic is similar to "making a mountain out of a molehill." You might use this tactic if you have a big issue that is not going the way you want it to and you need a way to derail it until you can get a counterproposal together. The best way is to find a small flaw in it and exploit it until it is withdrawn.

I was forced to use this tactic when the company I was working for decided to buy a computerized Material Requirements Planning (MRP) system. It was a good idea, but the team leader selected by the president had never implemented an MRP system, and the whole project was doomed to failure. I was selected by my vice president to be a member of the implementation team, and I was determined to keep my career from going down the tubes with this disaster. I found a few flaws with the purchasing module of the system. Purchasing modules, like purchasing people, are always vulnerable. By talking to the purchasing people and telling them what they were about to get, the flaws grew in magnitude until there were serious questions about the ability of the system to meet my company's needs. Since the president had already committed himself to the system and had tied my vice president's incentive compensation bonus to its successful implementation, I was able to get myself removed from the team in return for my silence on the system's flaws. They sent me into purchasing where I worked until they started to implement the purchasing module. I got what I wanted and so did my vice president. I wanted off the team. He wanted his fat bonus.

This technique is used all the time by the big boys when they want more time to study a problem before they make a decision. They usually like the concept, but they're not sure how their boss will like it. By delaying a decision, they have time to check out the boss's attitude or gain additional support from others at their level. I use this tactic, and it has helped me many times in getting what I want.

Diversion of Attention

Never let the other fellow set the agenda.
JAMES BAKER (b. 1930)

Have you ever watched a magician? They really don't make the things do what you think they do, do they? Do they really make scarfs disappear, or pull rabbits out of a hat? Of course not! What they do is divert your attention. Master Corporate Politicians do the same thing. When you want to talk about something they don't want to talk about, do you know what you and he talk about? You talk about what he wants to talk about. It isn't that he isn't interested, he's just not ready to talk about it.

You may find yourself in the same boat and need a way not to talk about something. I try to carry around in my memory at least two items that each of my peers is interested in, and the same for each of the honchos that are one level above me.

Keeping track of what interests my staff and their subordinates is tougher. I avoid conversations with them until they've talked to their supervisors, which gives me time to prepare an appropriate response. The most valued items are things I know will get their attention and get them talking.

Remember in the introduction of the book, I said that being a Master Corporate Politician was like playing king of the mountain. Know who is king and also know who isn't but would like to be. Have some ready diversional material ready for both. Keep track of job openings in the local area—everybody's interested in who's hiring and what they're paying.

The best example of this tactic was when a group of congressional investigators came to talk to us about a subject we knew we were in trouble on. Our company sent us a man with a contracts background who interviewed us for three days prior to the congressional investigators' arrival. When they came, the contracts guy did all the talking and didn't say a word about the subject of the investigation. He talked about everything in the world but that. When he got a pointed question, he dodged it gracefully and talked for ten minutes on another subject. We passed the investigation.

Have you ever noticed the real politicians—the ones in Washington? When a reporter asks them about a particular subject, and you know they don't want to talk about it, you can see them talk about what they do want to talk about. Very few reporters can keep them on track.

What good does it do to talk about what you want to? It allows you to control the conversation and stall the topic until you're ready to talk about it. Picking the time and place to fight a battle and choosing when to bring up a subject are tools that will help you in your career.

 ## Summary

Stalling is a very effective tool that Master Corporate Politicians use to get what they want. If Master Corporate Politicians aren't ready to make a decision, need time to postpone it, or would just rather wait a while, they stall. They tell you that they will get back to you, and they never do. They suggest that you get together, but they never get together with you. They bury ideas in committees, and afterwards, when pinned down, they will agree to a specific set of action, then not do them. They constantly find major problems with ideas they don't agree with, and they are very adept at diverting your attention. Master Corporate Politicians stall to get their way. This chapter has shown you some of the tactics they use to do that. Be warned!

chapter 5

Getting the Wolves Off Your Scent

What do you do when you know you're going to fail in a particular assignment or job? Usually, you know long before anyone else does, and you're forced to carry the burden alone until such time as the ax falls. No more. In this chapter, I'll show you tactics that will ensure you don't become a casualty of your own failures. Everyone fails, but not everyone winds up being ground into hamburger.

The best way to avoid being eaten for failure is to be almost done—lip of the cup. If failure is a surety, then the Master Corporate Politician will disassociate herself from the failure, fireproof her boss to the failure, use numbers to confuse her attackers, seek assistance with the priorities, write CYA memos, and create Pearl-Harbor files. Last, the Master Corporate Politician might hear only what she wants to hear—*I never knew!* Or, she will tell management what they want to hear—*there is no failure*. Watch them, they are tricky.

Lip of the Cup

All of us failed to match our dreams of perfection. So I rate us on the basis of our splendid failure to do the impossible.

WILLIAM FAULKNER (1897–1962)

Today's managers like to use a management style they consider participative. They like to feel that their management style represents the best of McGregor's theory *Y* manager—the one who cares more about people than about the organization. This method works well as long as the boss is reasonable and knowledgeable about the task when he uses the participative management style. Depending on the personality of the manager, problems arise when the manager is trying to be participative but the subordinate states that the task cannot be done because (insert excuse) or cannot be done on time. Participative managers don't like to hear, "It can't be done," or "We can't make that schedule." The subordinate runs the risk, when he's honest with his boss, of being branded as negative, or something other than a team player—either of which are career limiting.

When confronted with an unreasonable schedule for the accomplishment of a particular task or of many tasks, which combined make the on-time accomplishment of them impossible, use the Lip-of-the-cup method. The Lip-of-the-cup method, a method of responding participatively, has been used successfully by data-processing departments for years. When was the last time any data processing project was completed on time or within cost budget? Never! How do these guys get away with it when the poor purchasing guy or production control guy gets his head handed to him if he misses a single date? The answer is Lip of the cup responses to any question. An example of this type of dialogue:

Manager: I need this project finished by the end of the month. When do you guys think it can be done? (Note the participative style.)

Data Processing Type: I think we can do it by then if we don't run into any major hiccups. (Note that the data-processing type has *fireproofed* (found on page 71) the answer in case of failure—key phrase was "if we don't run into any major hiccups.")

When the end of the month comes:

Manager: The project's not finished. You guys said it would be done by now.

Data-Processing Type: We would have been done on schedule but for (insert excuse here). We should be done by the end of next week if we don't run into any more unforeseen problems.

Guess what? When the next week comes, they'll repeat the process. The success of this tactic lies in creating new, plausible excuses for each failure to meet schedule, and being almost finished—Lip of the cup—whenever queried on the subject.

The application of this tactic is telling unreasonable bosses whatever they want to hear. They'll believe you *and* be happy with you. All you have to do is keep a list of acceptable excuses available at all times. As the project or assignment progresses, keep a keen eye out for reasons on which to blame the failure. Keep careful notes of whom you talked to and their failure to perform. Examples:

I would've finished but Joe Blow didn't keep his promise to complete the _____ by _____. He now promises to supply

me with it by _____ and if he does, I think I can complete by
_____.

The assignment almost completed on schedule, but the beancounters cut back on the overtime. Our schedule assumed we could work all the OT we wanted. Just using straight time, I think we can complete by _____.

The key to success with the Lip-of-the-cup tactic is being eager and plausible. You represent yourself as a team player who is working hard to meet the objectives of the manager or organization, and if only someone or something else hadn't failed, you would have pulled it off.

Disassociation

Our failings sometimes bind us to one another as closely as could virtue itself.

LUC VAUVENARGUES, MARQUIS DE (1715–47)

When you're assigned a job that's impossible or is just too big for you, and you know it, then it's time to practice the tactic called disassociation. As Clint Eastwood said in several of his movies, "A man's got to know his limitations." Very wise advice. When you know you're going to fail, it's time to start recovery actions. The sooner you know and recognize it, the better—it gives you more time to prepare. Early recognition of failure, or the high probability of it, calls for a tactic I call disassociation. It's a clever technique that has saved my career many times.

Disassociation is keeping distance between you and the problem. The farther away you are from the problem, the less likely you are to be touched by its failure. There are several ways successful Master Corporate Politicians use this tactic. The first and the most common method of doing it is by assigning a matrix manager to the problem. The matrix manager, working for you, is assigned all the responsibility for the problem. It's his or her job to solve the problem by using the other members of your staff. If he or she succeeds, you can quickly rush in and grab all the glory. If he or she fails, the matrix manager takes the fall, not you. In failure or impending failure, you can replace the matrix manager, and the problem goes on until it's time to kill the replacement. You can replace matrix managers for quite a while. Being a matrix manager does have a down side.

Here is an example of how to use disassociation—and how it can backfire. I was hired into a company as a matrix manager. I knew I was hired to either fix the problems or die a slow, agonizing death. The director of material who hired me was trying to disassociate himself from a problem that was too big for him. I did the best I could to fix the problem, but the director and his staff wouldn't respond to my suggestions. The other director I was assigned to support recognized my efforts and, in a move that I have never seen before or since, took the material-management responsibilities for his program away from the director of material. He gave them to me! The director of material forgot one thing—too much distance indicates lack of interest. The disassociation tactic can backfire if not managed correctly.

I took over the material management of that program. It had been grossly mismanaged for several years. The material shortages were shutting down production lines daily. I assigned a shortage-control manager to respond to the factory on all shortages. It was an impossible task and I knew I was killing him when I assigned him to it, but it was going to take me at least six months to clean up the prior management's screwups and get the organization functioning. I needed a man to be recognized as responsible for this problem—and he was, since he was part of the management team that had screwed it up—until I could get it fixed. If the program director or other members of senior management had associated me with the shortage problem, they would have fired me before I had a chance to fix it. The man I selected took the assignment and did the best he could. He bought me time, but it killed his career with the company—I was never able to give him another significant assignment. I fixed the problems and became a hero, but my matrix manager was sacrificed. Cruel, you say? The guy probably should have been fired when they fired his boss, but they left that task to me. I took him and, rather than firing him, used him to help the organization, and me. He stayed with and retired from that company.

Why did he get crippled? When shortages or any other project or assignment gets out of control, management starts looking for someone to blame for failure. In this particular incident, he took all the heat from management—he explained all the failures that weren't explainable. Whoever did it would have died, and I chose to let them take my matrix manager instead of me. I feel bad about it, but he was part of the original problem. From my perspective, it was either him or me.

Disassociation is a very effective tool in buying you time to either find another job or to fix a problem. It can backfire on you as it did on my former boss—I think he was on tap to be promoted and had brought me in to buy him time, but I didn't buy him enough. Disassociation can keep you alive when you're faced with a situation where you know you're going to get burned.

I have three matrix managers working for me now. I keep on top of what they're doing and keep close contact with the other individuals they report to. I think disassociation is an excellent tool. When things go bad with one of the programs my matrix managers are assigned to, I can reprimand the matrix manager, I can replace him or her, or I can fix the problem—it's my choice. Another thing the disassociation tactic provides is dilution. The more levels of management a problem goes through, the less intense it becomes; just talking about it seems to dilute its intensity. By the time it gets to me, the problem has lost most of its emotional steam, and I can react to it rationally.

Fireproofing

When we turn to one another for counsel we reduce the number of our enemies.

KAHLIL GIBRAN (1883–1931)

They have a term in legal circles called contributory negligence. In large corporations, it's called fireproofing. Fireproofing means that the more people you get to agree with a decision, the less heat you're going to receive if it turns out bad. In application, particularly if you're still low on the totem pole, it means getting your boss's prior approval before taking a risky action.

Sound easy? No way! Getting a Master Corporate Politician to agree to a risk in advance is nearly impossible—they're not stupid. They know if they agree to something and it turns out bad, their management will think they screwed up, and Master Corporate Politicians don't screw up—someone else does. Their preference will be to let you move out and do it. If it's good, they'll grab the glory. If it's bad, they'll lead the pack in putting the rope around your neck.

How do you combat this? You can always ask for direction. If and when you don't receive it, just wait and ask again. Keep notes of these conversations. You can afford to wait longer than he can because he's the boss, and he's responsible. If it fails and he starts the inquisition—let's punish someone for this—you can prove you tried to get resolution and your boss failed to give it to you. Wait him out, he'll come around. It doesn't hurt to let others know you tried to obtain a decision and failed. The more people who know of a problem, the sooner there will be a resolution.

Fireproofing is also insulating yourself from failure. Such phrases as, "If I don't run into any obstacles," or "If everything goes my way," or "If So and So comes through as promised," tend to mitigate any failure on your part because your commitment was based on a set of parameters that didn't happen. Be sure to add as many assumptions to any commitment as you can. The more you add, the more excuses you have for failure.

Another tactic I learned while in the army is, "If he didn't tell me not to do it, then he approved my action." This is almost an axiom. If you tell your boss you're going to do something, and he doesn't say no to it, he's effectively given you approval. Therefore, I make it a habit of telling my boss of every controversial action I intend to make. Usually, he doesn't fully understand the implications of what I'm doing, or why I'm telling him. I document the discussion in my personal diary and if the action went badly, I remind him that he gave me tacit approval to proceed. It's hard to deny when a person tells you of the date and time of a particular conversation and shows you written evidence of it.

Number Dazzle

I always divide people into two groups. Those who live by what they know to be a lie, and those who live by what they believe, falsely, to be the truth.

CHRISTOPHER HAMPTON (b. 1946)

When you see a set of numbers, particularly if it's a computer printout, you believe it, right? I used to. Don't—a computer is only as good as the data fed into it, and the people that feed them are Master Corporate Politicians, and they lie. As I've already mentioned, Master Corporate Politicians do lie, and they use their computers to do it for them.

What's a number dazzle? A number dazzle is when you throw so many numbers at a boss he concedes his position in favor of yours. It isn't that he understands the numbers—systems have become so complicated that even the bean counters don't always understand them—it's just that he trusts them. Numbers don't lie, right? Wrong! There's a saying, "Liars figure, and figures lie." It's true, but most bosses don't know it. Many sneaky Master Corporate Politicians use a computer to help them disguise a disaster when they need to buy time. When they get caught, they can always blame it on the computer.

The best example of a number dazzle was early in my career when I was the division accounting manager of a large electronics firm. The division I was working for was losing lots of money. We were poorly managed and trying to compete with the Japanese and Koreans, and we were losing badly. The corporate vice president looked over the books prior to closing us down forever. We spent three days going over the books and then started to put together a story that would tell the board of directors we could get well within three months and we shouldn't be sacrificed. When the vice president showed me his final numbers, I told him he was "full of shit" and the numbers were no good. His response was, "No one knows they're no good except you, and if you don't tell, then I won't. You want to work here, or not?" I got the message. He took the numbers back to the corporate office and we didn't get fried.

I used the same logic many times afterwards. No one knows if my numbers are any good, except me. I'll pad them if I need to. The number dazzle works particularly well in combination with fireproofing. If your numbers are based on assumptions, and those assumptions turn out to be different from the facts, and they always are, no one can blame you if the numbers are off.

Another variant of the number dazzle is overwhelming them with facts. Managers can usually handle only a few numbers in their heads at one time. Overload them! If you do, they'll ask you to interpret the numbers for them. You will, as a good Master Corporate Politician, interpret them accurately, right? Managers have become lazy—they expect someone to digest everything for them and tell them how to interpret it. Take advantage of it!

 Priority Control

> When people are taken out of their depths they lose their
> heads, no matter how charming a bluff they may put up.
> F. SCOTT FITZGERALD (1896–1940)

Got fifty pounds of work your management wants you to do with a workforce stressed for only thirty pounds? Happens every day, right? It does to me, and I'm sure I pass it down. It seems to me they want a Cadillac and are willing to pay for only a GEO. How do you combat the impending failure? You can't do all that's required of you, and you know you're going to fail. How do you save yourself?

I call it priority control. I go to my boss, also a Master Corporate Politician, and ask for help. I tell him I can't get it all done and something is going to have to slip. Without fail, his first reaction is always to put the staff on overtime, but I've already had them on overtime for the past few weeks. We're still not going to meet every objective. If he's a good politician, he tells me to handle it the best I can. If he's a good boss, he sits down and we discuss our mutual understanding of the priorities and what the impact will be if we miss one of them. Jointly, we determine which will slip and which won't. A good Master Corporate Politician will not commit himself to any priority scheme—what if he's wrong? If you're lucky, you might get the number-one item, but don't count on getting any help after that. Try anyway, and write down the results of the effort.

What do you do? Write it down that you asked and then refer to the section on fireproofing (especially tacit approval). When you let the boss know you're writing everything down, and he knows you asked for help identifying priorities and are writing it down, he will be very careful in his responses to you.

Most bosses in the middle ranks aren't yet full Master Corporate Politicians. They're still human beings and they'll help you with priority control. The higher you get, the less help you can count on getting. When you reach full manager (50+ people) then you can count on no help. The guy you work for is trying to save his ass as hard as you are. Ask anyway and write it down—it may save your life later. This is such a significant topic to your survival, that I cover it from different perspectives in Chapters 13 and 14. It is an awesome tool of career destruction.

CYA: Cover Your Ass

We are responsible for actions performed in response to circumstances for which we are not responsible.
ALLAN MASSIE (b. 1938)

If you haven't figured out the title of this section, it means covering yourself with paper—similar to fireproofing, but done with paper and used when someone other than your boss is involved. It can be used on the boss, but it tends to make him or her angry if you resort to it.

How does it work? Simply, it means you write a letter to the guy who's not performing, telling him he isn't and what course of action you feel is appropriate. One of two things will happen. First, he might ignore you. If he does, then wait an appropriate amount of time and send him another letter. He may still ignore you, but this is okay because when the inquisition starts, you have written evidence proving you tried to get it fixed and the dummy you sent the letters to didn't do anything about it.

The second action that may result is that the guy will get off his lazy butt and go fix it, but if he's a Master Corporate Politician, don't count on it; or, he'll most likely send you back a letter saying it isn't his fault and he can't fix it because of _____, or he'll fix it after _____ happens. The typical Master Corporate Politician will toss the blame to some other department and do it with a letter. He may or may not copy the department he's blaming (which I cover in Chapter 11), but he'll toss the blame elsewhere. If he does, you start the whole procedure all over.

The objective of this section is to let you know that you need to have evidence proving you tried to get the problem fixed, and you need to keep that evidence close at hand. When a problem gets big enough or bad enough, someone in top management is going to get involved and will want to know why the subordinate managers haven't fixed it already. He pays them to fix problems, and when one reaches his level it means his staff let him down.

Most Master Corporate Politicians know what you're doing when you do this. They do it all the time themselves. When they get a letter, they know the ramifications of not doing something. When you get one, either fix the problem or write a letter blaming the problem on someone else. Save the copies of your letters.

Pearl Harbor Files

He that is born to be hanged shall never be drowned.
FRENCH PROVERB (14TH CENTURY)

A close cousin to the previous section on CYA is the Pearl Harbor file. I think the Pearl Harbor file got its name from General George Marshall of World War II fame. He supposedly wrote a letter to the commander of Pearl Harbor telling him that the island should be on alert for an attack and the defenses should be "beefed up." He wrote the letter long before the attack by the Japanese.

Common usage has defined it to mean that you keep a file on everyone that lists all the screw-ups and anything else you can put your dirty little hands on. Why? You may need it if something goes wrong, or if the individual comes after you. The CYA letters, the recordings in your diary, copies of letters relating to the subject, and anything else that may be of benefit should be saved.

How do you use a Pearl Harbor file? Carefully. I write down everything that happens in my life in my diary, and when I fill up the book, I load the references into my computer database program. It gives me a listing by person, date, and subject. That and my correspondence file are about all I need. It makes a very strong argument when you can tell the scalp hunters you talked to Joe Blow fourteen times on the subject and wrote him sixteen letters trying to get him to fix a particular problem. The scalp they take won't be yours.

The Boy Scout motto is *Be Prepared*. With a Pearl Harbor file, you will be.

Hear What You Want To

> The opposite of talking isn't listening. The opposite of talking is waiting.
>
> FRAN LEBOWITZ (b. 1951)

Management has tunnel vision a great deal of the time. Management, in most instances, got to be management by having some skills and experience, and they judge what they hear based on their experience base. If they have no background in a subject, then they tend not to put as much credence on your telling them the sky is falling as they would if they've had a previous experience where the sky did fall on them. If they don't want to hear it or they can't understand it, why waste your time telling them?

Am I suggesting you don't tell your management the sky is falling? Of course not. I'm telling you they may not hear or understand you, and therefore it's important that you document that you did tell them. They'll tell you to work a little harder and put more people on it—standard Master Corporate Politician responses—but they may not really understand the impact.

A good example of this occurred a few years ago. I was put in charge of a study to tell one of our largest customers how much it would cost my company if they were to cancel our long-term contract. My vice president, a Master Corporate Politician under pressure from his boss, told his boss that he would have a number in three weeks. I immediately told my vice president that it was impossible to do the task on time, but he didn't hear me. I told him again a week later and a week after that. When three weeks were up, he asked for the number, and I told him I didn't have it—that it would take at least three months, and even then, the number wouldn't withstand an audit because the bills of material and inventory balances were inaccurate. He told me to clean them up and give him a number. I told him that to do that would take a year or more.

He listened to me, but heard only that it would take three months to give him a number. In three months, and under pressure, I gave the vice president the number. It was large and generally not supportable because the bills of material were about 50 percent accurate and the inventory records were less accurate than that. Throughout the three months, we met weekly and discussed progress. He wanted me to say I was making progress and that I could get the job done in three months. I told him what he wanted to hear, and I also told him that the numbers wouldn't be any good. He heard only what he wanted to and passed the numbers on to the vice president of finance anyway. The audit came, and we failed.

The postmortem went this way:

Vice President: Why didn't you tell me the numbers weren't any good?

Me: I did. Many times, and particularly when I gave you the numbers.

Vice President: Bullshit, you did!

Me: I can prove it to you. (I pulled out my diary and showed him by date the record of our conversations.)

Vice President: Okay, so you told me. I didn't hear you. You should have made me listen.

Me: I tried, but maybe I should have tried harder.

Always let the big guys off the hook when you can. If you say, even with a Master Corporate Politician's tact, "You screwed up all by yourself," then they'll hate your guts for it.

 # Tell Them What They Want to Hear

> *Men are not to be told anything they might find too painful; the secret depths of human nature, the sordid physicalities, might overwhelm or damage them.*
> **MARGARET ATWOOD** (b. 1939)

As in the previous section, management wants to hear what they want to hear. If you tell them something that's different from that, you run the risk of having them bite your head off or not listen to you. You may also run the risk of being considered someone with a bad attitude who can't get with the program. As a Master Corporate Politician, you can turn this to your advantage.

If you know your boss is in a war with the engineering department, present a problem to him or her so the engineers are mostly to blame. It may be a joint screw-up, but if it's presented so the engineering department appears to be more than 50 percent at fault, he or she will hear your problem and give you support in its resolution. If you try to present a fair picture of the problem, notice how the boss's questions lead you to say it's primarily an engineering screw-up. Master Corporate Politicians are aware of this, and you should be too.

Bosses don't like to hear that their organizations are screwed up. So what do you tell them? You tell them what they want to hear and subtly let them know they need to fix something. Here's an example:

You: Boss, you really have a great warehouse organization.

Boss: Yeah, I do. I personally picked each one of those guys, and they do a great job.

You: I've never seen such an efficient organization. They must process thousands of parts a day.

Boss: I sometimes wonder myself how they do it.

You: You know that production control's unhappy about the way they're handling the line-stop parts? If those guys could just understand how much you do for them.

Boss: I've just about given up on making those guys happy.

You: I wish they would appreciate what you do for them.

Boss: I guess I need to look into the line-stop thing and see if there isn't something we could do better. What do you think?

You: It might help calm the storm. If I told them you were looking at it, then they might not go to the vice president.

What did you just do? You communicated with your boss—you told her the warehouse people were all screwed up, and you also told her what she wanted to hear, which was, "They're great." What did you do? You got her to fix a problem.

Telling the boss what he or she wants to hear may sometimes be smarter than telling him or her the truth. Use this tactic with care, but be aware of it because your own employees may try to use it on you. Regardless of how often you tell them you want the truth and nothing but the truth, they'll interpret your foul mood one day as a signal that you really didn't want to hear it. Be aware!

 ## Summary

Failure comes to the best of us. We all fail, or we haven't tried to do anything. When you see it coming, and you should be able to do that after reading this book, you need to round up your excuses and reasons why you have failed. You now know nine different ways to survive when you see failure is imminent. You know that lip of the cup works just about every time, provided you don't overuse it. You know about disassociation, fireproofing, number dazzle, priority control, CYA letters, and Pearl Harbor files. Master Corporate Politicians will hear what they want and will tell management what they want to hear. Be aware because the Master Corporate Politicians will use them on you every chance they get.

chapter 6

Be a Scavenger, But Look Like a Hunter

If you haven't figured it out by now, failures require solutions and the solutions have to appear to be reasonable and stand a good chance of success. Some of the more commonly used solutions that rarely solve a problem but give the user more time to seek a real solution are listed in this chapter. The oldest trick in the book is a reorganization. If that doesn't satisfy the attackers, the Master Corporate Politician will buy a new computer system, or create tiger teams. When the budget is being overrun, the Master Corporate Politician will just redo the budget. Overtime is the Master Corporate Politician's answer to just about every impending failure.

Keep in mind another cardinal rule, a Master Corporate Politician never fails. Even when he fails, he doesn't fail. These tactics are listed because you may actually fail, and you need a solution that will give your attackers a reason to keep you on the payroll. Using these tactics prior to failure should also be considered.

Reorganize

Most of the change we think we see in life
Is due to truths being in and out of favor.

ROBERT FROST (1874–1963)

By the time you reach middle management, you will be familiar with this tactic. In fact, I was in one organization that used it so often that one of my peers told me, "If you don't like the current organizational structure, don't worry. We'll reorganize again next month, and we'll get another one. We call it the organization-of-the-month club." He was right. In the year I was in that organization, I went through four bosses and a half a dozen different reporting changes.

What advantage does changing an organization chart have? It allows the person owning the chart to tell whoever is looking at it that he:

1. Has realigned his staff to meet a new problem, or

2. Has put the right person in the job, finally, or

3. Has gotten rid of that incompetent guy who was screwing things up, or

4. Has put the troubled organization under one of his aces who will clean it up pronto, or

5. Has formed his organization into a natural work group that will be twice as productive, or

6. Has reorganized to prevent further hiring, or

7. Has created a spot for _____, who's the illegitimate son/daughter of the chairman of the board, or

8. Has done anything the listener wants him to have done.

I don't like change, and neither do most people. Why reorganize just to please someone else? You're not reorganizing for them—you're doing it for you. The reason you're reorganizing is because you failed, or know you're going to fail and you're trying to save your job, your career, your promotion, or whatever else could be impacted by your failure. You're reorganizing to show your boss or his boss that the only reason you failed was because your organization chart didn't have the right names in it, not because you're just no damned good. You're going to convince him that with the new organization chart, things are going to turn around and hum like an expensive Swiss watch.

Isn't it more practical to put an organization in place and let it run? Sure it is, but the one you got doing it, ain't doing it. It could be because of factors that have nothing to do with who sits in which seats, but management always believes that a new face can do better than an old one. It's as if they have more faith in an untried individual than they do in an experienced one. Why do you think professional recruiters make so much money? Management wants new faces.

Does unnecessary change disrupt and reduce efficiency? You bet your buttons it does. First, the employees don't like change, even when it's necessary. When it's not necessary, they can become hostile, and their morale and goodwill disappear. They often perceive the new management as political appointees and treat them as such. Do I reorganize? Yes sir! Every chance I get.

New System

Only man is not content to leave things as they are but must always be changing them, and when he has done so, is seldom satisfied with the result.

ELSPETH HUXLEY (b. 1907)

This tactic is so old I'm surprised it still works, but it does. Got a problem? Create a new computer or manual system to fix it. The person who's on your case about the problem will be satisfied that you're taking corrective action.

It works so well, it's used by all levels of management to fix just about any problem. Some examples of how this tactic have been used are as follows:

Problem: Production is behind schedule.

Master Corporate Politician's Solution: Introduce a computerized work in process system to track where everything is located so it can get the proper priority.

Real Solution: Get out there and make the factory foremen follow the existing priority system.

Problem: Purchasing is always buying the wrong thing.

Master Corporate Politician's Solution: Implement a new requirements system to tell them what they need to buy.

Real Solution: Make engineering clean up the bills of material and manufacturing scheduling tell procurement when they really want it.

Problem: Inventory accuracy is horrible.

Master Corporate Politician's Solution: Buy some new

inventory control software to give us real-time inventory accuracy.

Real Solution: Make the stock keepers accountable for accuracy and punish those that fail.

Problem: We never know we're losing money until it's too late to fix it.

Master Corporate Politician's Solution: Implement a new computerized cost-accounting system to give us real-time cost data and allow us to make quick decisions.

Real Solution: Have the accountants publish data more frequently. The once-a-month reporting that normally comes out is done more for the financial community than for the manufacturer.

As you can see from the preceeding examples, there's a new system solution to every problem. New systems carry with them none of the problems that burden the existing ones.

Everything will be okay as soon as we get this new system installed. What are the problems with this solution? Several, but most people don't know them. The prime problem is data—the computer is only as good as the data fed into it. As the data-processing types say, "Garbage in, garbage out." Why is this a problem? It's a problem because in most instances, there is an existing system that is trying to function with bad data, and the proposed systems solution will suffer because the data fed into the new system is also defective.

Have you ever tried to implement a new system? It's just as hard as I imagine having a baby is—I can't say for sure because I was born the wrong sex, but I can say it's the most painful experience you can have in a nondata-processing career. Nothing seems to go according to plan, regardless of the quality of the planning. Common problems that happen with every system implementation are

- Data get screwed up.

- The programs don't work.

- They work, but the application was wrong.

- The users of the programs don't like them.

- Minor flaws in programing logic don't appear until they've screwed up the data.

- The users continue to use the old system.

- Key personnel quit or leave, and the whole thing goes down the tube.

There are lots of reasons why systems implementations are such a pain in the butt, but the most prevalent reason is that most of the time the implementation effort is a failure. One in seven systems implementations fail—they fail to meet the stated objectives and therefore spawn another generation of new systems.

How do you combat this tactic? Simple, you start by asking questions. "How much is this going to cost, and what's the payback?" Also ask, "Do you have an existing system, and what would it take to bring it up to speed?" Another question that causes the Master Corporate Politician to start tap dancing is, "What's the accuracy of the data in the existing system, and what makes you think the accuracy will be better in the new one?"

Systems rarely have any form of payback analysis performed prior to the start of their implementation. Why? The answer is that they were suggested as a solution to a problem that must be fixed at all costs. If an astute manager analyzes why the existing system is failing, the cost to fix it might be considerably less than implementing a brand-new one—particularly since one in seven fail and create further opportunities to use this tactic.

The application of this tactic follows this path. Your boss or some other big shot is after you for a failure. You responded with the following, "We're studying the implementation of a new system that will fix all of our problems." This gives you a month or so to fix the underlying problem. If you do, then you report that you've determined to stay with the existing system. If you don't, you say you're now looking at the cost of fixing the existing system versus the cost of scrapping it and implementing a new one. That'll give you another month. If it can't be fixed in another month, you as a Master Corporate Politician might have to start to implement a new system. Don't worry if it fails because you've assigned a matrix manager to implement it, and when it does, it was his fault (see The Auction, page 34). Pick another matrix manager and start over again. When this tactic fails for about the third or fourth time, it may be time to suggest that you need a different system. While all of this is going on, get your butt in gear and go fix the underlying problem that caused the existing system to fail.

There are many variations of the tactics in this chapter. Let me relate a classic case. I was once at a program review with a critical supplier and they used these tactics on me with some success because I was still young and naive. In my initial contact with the supplier, he told me the reason he wasn't delivering to my purchase-order schedule was because his factory was poorly laid out. Once he got it reorganized, he would be able to spit out my units as if they were popcorn. I listened to his plan of reorganization, and his new facility layout. I was impressed. It sounded good, and it was believable. The supplier implemented the new layout, and production didn't increase any—it was the same.

When I returned three months later, I found out the reason for his inability to deliver. The underlying problem with his factory was parts shortages. What did he tell me then? He told me he was implementing a new computer system that would allow him to get his parts to the factory floor in time to meet my delivery needs. Still young and innocent, I bought it—things did not improve.

Three months later, I returned again, and guess what? They were now going to give me an organization change. The old management "just wasn't worth a shit" and the new management would cure all the problems associated with my order. Guess what? They stayed behind schedule until I found another source for their part and cancelled their order. Now they practice corporate politics on some other innocent buyer who hasn't read this book.

 # Tiger Teams

> *Some great men owe most of their greatness to the ability of detecting in those they destine for their tools the exact quality of strength that matters for their work.*
>
> **JOSEPH CONRAD** (1857–1924)

Want to make your management think you're a real hero? Put a tiger team together to fix a problem. It doesn't matter whose problem it is, suggest a team be assembled to go fix it.

Management will love it! You need to understand that management likes stupid ideas like this because they give the world the illusion that something is being done to fix a prob-

BE A SCAVENGER, BUT LOOK LIKE A HUNTER

lem. To illustrate how management loves stupid ideas, a friend of mine was assigned to a systems implementation group against his will. The tiger team consisted of about ten guys located in four different buildings scattered all over the city. He and I got to drinking one night, and I suggested he recommend that management buy a double-wide trailer and locate the entire team together. We laughed at the idea, but management bought it and put the trailer out in the parking lot, but never added any toilet facilities. The team never used it.

Management loves a tiger team to fix anything—it has such a wholesome look to it: "I've put a select team together to go study this problem and to fix it." It has a ring of truth that indicates the manager is actively working the problem, but it can be used as a ruse to stall (see Let's Put a Committee Together, page 57). Generally, though, a tiger team is put together to solve a problem, not to stall.

Whom do you put on tiger teams? I put the young college graduates and other people that are idealistic on them. If you put seasoned pros on the team, they'll give you whatever answer they think you want to hear. Why? Because they aren't stupid. If they know you have a preconceived idea of how a problem should be solved, they'll agree with you rather than forging new ground. It makes sense because they're confirming what the boss thinks, and they don't have to risk incurring his or her wrath with an idea that he or she may not like. If they suggest a new and radical idea and it fails, then they're blamed. Idealistic people don't think like this and are more interested in getting the job done. They make the assumption that the boss put them on the team to actually fix a problem. They also assume the boss has no idea of how to fix it, or he or she would already have done it.

What do you do if you're assigned to a tiger team? Know your boss. If he's the kind of guy that uses these teams as a collective rubber stamp for his ideas, then give him his ideas. If he's the kind of guy who's genuinely seeking a novel solution, then try to give him one.

Should you be glad to be assigned to one of these teams? Maybe. In several locations where I've worked management puts the deadwood people that have fallen from favor or are not productive on teams to keep them busy. They can't fire them, and they can't put them to work. What do they do with them? Put them on tiger teams and hope they quit. Other places where I've worked, the opposite is true. The teams are staffed with high potential barn burners to give them exposure and experience. It all depends on the management of the particular company and its philosophy.

As part of a tiger team, one thing to remember is that volume indicates worth. When you make your report, start it with a two-page management summary—it's all they'll read anyway. Make the rest of the report long and involved. A ten-page report carries none of the weight of a two-volume, hundred-thousand-word report. Footnotes indicate research and precision in your thought. How do you get the volume? Record everything that could possibly be recorded. Report in detail every conversation with every individual, copious notes on all meetings, copies of complete reports that are referenced, and anything else that might have a bearing on the subject of the report.

If you're the boss, then a tiger team will buy you time and may even give you a solution to a problem. Have you ever noticed that all the Presidents of the United States use select committees? If they really wanted a solution, they would implement the recommendations of their tiger teams, but do they? Rarely. The President uses his tiger teams for show, to make the voters think he cares about an issue, and to buy himself some time until the issue goes away, or he can think of a solution he's satisfied with. Whenever he's asked what he's doing about a problem, he can say, "I have this tiger team/select committee studying the problem and when they finish, then I'll have a solution." Was that an acceptable answer? It's been working for years.

Tiger teams are a useful tool in explaining what you're doing to fix a problem. The listener is generally happy with the response, and it gives the Master Corporate Politician the time to figure out what he's really going to do to fix the problem. Tiger teams are also a place to dump people in your organization whom you want to get rid of and a place to groom future hotshots. I recommend you use a lot of tiger teams, particularly when you have a problem that your management is going to crucify you for if you don't get it fixed.

Redo the Budgets/Forecasts

You can fool all the people all the time if the advertising is right and the budget is big enough.
JOSEPH E. LEVINE (b. 1905)

Budget failure means one of several things. It could mean you were no good in forecasting your requirements, or it could mean you didn't manage your department as you should have, or it means something, or lots of little somethings, happened that forced the budget to go out of control. Which one did it? You better have an answer.

What do you do when you know you're not going to make the budget, and you know someone from finance is going to come looking for you with a machete? Does it mean you start looking for a job? Do you start looking for someone to blame it on, or do you redo the budget? Either one, but this section deals with the latter.

Budgets are tools created by management to maintain control over the operations of their facility/operation. As discussed previously (see Negotiation Basics, page 39), when you submit a budget, it will always be cut by the accountants and then again by the top brass. When you submit one, pad the hell out of it. Budgets are one of the ways management uses to beat the stuffing out of you. No one ever underruns all the items on the budget, so it gives the big boys something to get angry about—they love to pick at you on a line-item basis. If you're smart, you'll see to it that your bottom-line actuals are less than your bottom-line budget. Failure to do this will cause you to be a candidate for the next purge.

Depending on the company, I've seen budgets used as weapons and I've seen them damn near ignored. Both of these approaches are nonproductive. A budget should be monitored and adhered to, and a smart Master Corporate Politician, regardless of the management practices, will do just that. You can never tell when there will be a management change.

How do you get relief if you're blowing the budget? It helps to have a friend in accounting. Failing that, the only way to do it effectively is to maintain copious records of anything that caused you to fail. It also helps, when you submit a budget, that you do it based on a set of assumptions. When any one of the assumptions doesn't happen, or happens to a greater extreme than you planned, you have an excuse to reopen the budget process. When you've blown the budget, or know you're going to, it helps if you kept records of why. You can go to the vice president and show him how you've blown it, and why. If you can't do that, then you'll be labeled an ineffective manager—and you know what happens to them.

At least once a week, I sit down for fifteen minutes and think about plausible excuses for me to overrun a budget. I keep a running list of those excuses in the front of my diary. I also have at least one and sometimes two people on my staff who do nothing but monitor the budget and record the real reasons for failure. I don't tell my management the truth, but I know, and I punish those who screw up. Those budget people are also chartered with collecting data for me to use in the event I get trapped in a budget war. I tell them if I have to chop anything out of my budget, it will be them, which seems to give them a tremendous amount of motivation in keeping my affairs in order. I usually have more data than I need when the bean counters come after me.

I like to take what I call a prophylactic approach to budgeting. If I know I'm not going to make it, I like to tell the accounting manager or the vice president—depends on who has the power—long before he knows it himself. I tell him I'm not going to make it and why. This serves two purposes. First it shows the accounting manager or vice president that I'm a professional and I know what I'm doing—or at least gives that illusion. Second, it fireproofs him from coming after me later. He can't very well come after me when I went to him a month ago and told him I was in trouble and asked his advice on how to fix it, can he? Always ask the bean counters for their advice. They're like the data processing guys, narrow-minded with big egos. I can say that because I used to be a corporate controller and a data-processing manager.

Budgets are a pain in the butt. You need to spend a lot of time learning the process and managing it. Know when you're in trouble and put some of the Master Corporate

Politician's tactics to work to save yourself. Budget failure is one of the prime reasons managers involuntarily disappear in the night, or end up as a blue-light special at a management sale.

Work Overtime

It's true hard work never killed anybody, but I figure, why take the chance?

RONALD REAGAN (b. 1911)

Bosses really eat this one up. Nothing makes a boss think you're really trying than to see you and your staff working a lot of overtime. Why? Well, look at it from their perspective. If you failed, and you weren't working overtime when you did, then the argument is that if you had, you wouldn't have failed.

Another reason bosses like overtime is that it allows them to get a job done without additional hiring, which they hate. If you tell them the solution to your failure is additional people, then they're going to throw you out of their office. If the solution is working the lazy lowlifes a little harder, they'll smile and nod their heads. Overtime is one solution rarely objected to by management.

When asked why you haven't already started working overtime, or why you waited to fail before starting to work overtime, the answer should be that you thought you were going to succeed without it and you were trying to conserve the budget. Reasonable, right?

What do you do when you have been working overtime, lots of it, and you still fail? You failed because you just didn't have the staff to do the job. How do you sell more overtime?

The Master Corporate Politician's answer is that you don't need it—just start working smarter, not harder. A person who can't swim isn't going to stay alive any longer by thrashing harder. Get some help!

How do you handle a staff that has been working fifty to sixty hours per week for months and gets the word from you that there is no relief in sight and they'll have to continue for another month or two? How do you prevent them from lynching you from the nearest tree? Remember, you're a Master Corporate Politician and Master Corporate Politicians sometimes lie, or at least shade the truth; tell them it's almost over and relief is almost at hand. Try not to be specific, but if you get pinned down, specify a reasonable time—one you think they'll accept—and tell them it'll end then. When that time comes, do the same tactic over again (See Lip of the Cup, page 66).

Working overtime is one of the few tactics I know that works every time it's used—management eats it up, particularly if they aren't paying for it. Use it!

Summary

Nobody likes a loser. Nobody likes to hear excuses for failure. You failed, and that's that. If you do fail, don't admit it, but suggest a solution for the temporary disfunction. Suggesting or implementing a solution and telling everyone early, before the world comes to an end, may save your life and prevent the scalp hunters from looking for you. Consider a reorganization, a new system, tiger teams, redoing the budgets, or working your staff overtime. These tactics do work.

chapter 7

Saving Your Hide at Any Cost

Everybody fails—except a Master Corporate Politician. If you don't take risks, however, you'll not only fail, but you will not succeed. The world is owned by people who take risks and failed. The secret to your success will depend on damage control and how well you are able to blunt the association between you and the failure, or shift it to someone or something else.

This chapter deals with many useful tactics in siege defense. When you fail, the wolves will be after you, trying to rip your heart out. These tactics are useful survival techniques when all the previous tactics in this book have failed. Preventive medicine is much cheaper and more effective than trying to cure a disease—an ounce of prevention is worth a pound of cure. But sometimes, you need the cure.

Many Master Corporate Politicians never admit failure. Remember the cardinal rule, Master Corporate Politicians never fail. Some are honest and rely on management's goodwill. Many will shift focus from their failure to the failure of others. Some will blame their employees, or procurement, or data processing. Some will even claim that higher priorities were being followed, hence no failure.

It Ain't Failure

To get it right, be born with luck or else make it. Never give up. Get the knack of getting people to help you and also pitch in yourself. A little money helps, but what really gets it right is to never—I repeat—never under any conditions face the facts.

RUTH GORDON (b. 1896–1985)

By far the best answer for failure is to claim there was no failure. If you don't agree that there was a failure, then the proof of the alleged failure lies with your accuser. Proof is hard to come by when you use all the Master Corporate Politician's tricks.

Why deny failure? You deny it because once your name is associated with failure, you are labeled a loser. Losers never go anywhere. I've seen a lot of capable people who had one major failure, and they were sidelined and left there to die. One of the prices you must pay to be a success is to risk failure. If you fail, deny, with absolute conviction, that there was a failure.

Is it hard to prove a failure? You bet! Think about it in your own life. One of your children tells you a story you know is a lie. Can you prove it? Nope! What do you do? You grill the heck out of your kid and wind up either punishing the child anyway, or accepting the answer. It's the same way in a corporation. Your management may be sure you're lying, but if they can't prove it—and they rarely can—then they will generally accept your denial.

Honesty Is the Best Policy

Nothing astonishes men so much as common sense and plain dealing.

RALPH WALDO EMERSON (1803–82)

If you know you can't successfully deny it, admit it. Honesty may save you from the boneyard, depending on the type of boss you have. Some bosses will accept failure, as I have, as part of your job. If they do, honesty is the only defense. If you're honest and loyal and your boss isn't a Master Corporate Politician, he'll probably try to save you. If he's a Master Corporate Politician and needs you in order to stay alive himself, he may also try to save you.

It's funny, but one time I failed miserably and confessed to my boss. Since he was also associated with my failure, we talked about it and he presented his management with a story that made me appear to have succeeded beyond all possible expectations. He also told them I still had some work to do to "clean it up," but the word to the bosses was that my failure was a success.

My boss accepted my failure and helped me. I've done this many times, but usually I do it a little bit at a time. I admit each small failure as it occurs; this way when the big failure occurs as a result of the series of the small ones, he's prepared and almost a party to my failure. Only on a few occasions have I been trashed and held totally accountable.

Honest people have a record of rising from the ashes and getting another chance—I have. Most successful Master Corporate Politicians have failed a few times and are willing to give you another chance after the smoke of your failure clears. It may take a year or so for it to clear, but if you like the company and are willing to wait, then be honest and admit your failure and don't try to assign it to anyone else. Even in those instances where the failure is a result of someone else's failure, it may be to your advantage to accept the blame.

I like honest people, and I trust them. I would much rather have an honest employee than one I was never completely sure of. I give honest people a second chance and so do most Master Corporate Politicians.

 # Shift Focus

The true art of memory is the art of attention.
SAMUEL JOHNSON (1709–84)

Let me give you an example of this tactic you can use tonight. I come home occasionally after going drinking with my buddies after work. My spouse is angry because I failed to call and tell her that I would be late. What's my response? I use this one all the time: "Look at this house! It's a trash heap. What did you do while I was gone?" What have I done? I shifted the focus of attention from my failure to call her to her failure to clean up the house. What do we talk about now? The failure shifted from me to her, and the discussion focuses on her failure, not mine. By the way, she uses this tactic on me now, too.

The following sections deal with the different ways to shift focus and how easy it is to divert attention from your failure to someone else's.

Shift Focus—Nonspecific

There's man all over for you, blaming on his boots the fault of his feet.

SAMUEL BECKETT (1906–89)

The best tactic is to shift focus to another department and hang the failure on them. This is contrasted to the other blame categories in that it is not specific. You are not attacking any individual, but rather an amorphous mass. Laying the blame on a department doesn't make a vicious enemy of the department manager; it may make her mad, but it may allow you to get away with your failure. You may be lucky and find an honest person running the department who will accept some or all of the blame.

The boilerplate example of the nonspecific shift tactic is to say, "My department did all it could, but _____ department let me down and didn't give me _____, which I needed to finish. When are they going to get their act together?" A specific example is, "The engineering was no good—it couldn't be bought, built, or inspected. When is engineering going to come out of their ivory tower and join the rest of the world?" Another, "We tried, but the schedule was no good—it was impossible. If we had good schedules, then we could do it. Why do we get these jobs with schedules that aren't any good?" A classic that usually works is, "Marketing, sales, contracts signed us up for something we couldn't do, and they never even asked us if we could. We tried our hardest, but we just couldn't do it. When are they going to start asking us?" A final example: "We were doing good—real good—until quality control started to rip us apart. We would've made it except for all the scrap QC made us redo or throw away. We'll never make anything in that shop as long as we've got these idiots inspecting us. When are they going to get some inspectors who know what they're doing?"

I hope you noticed that you pulled the blame off yourself and placed it on another organization with a question. The question at the end of each excuse is the key. You failed, but you ask a question to your accusers that shifts the attention from your failure to the organization that caused you to fail. Management has a mind like a child—it has a short attention span. The successful Master Corporate Politician uses every opportunity to make the attention shift from him or her to anything else.

 # Blame Your Employees

As soon as men know that they can kill without fear of punishment or blame, they kill; or at least they encourage killers with approving smiles.
SIMONE WEIL (1909–43)

Whenever there is a failure, the immediate response of management is to find someone to blame it on and then to punish him or her for it. One of my least favorite tactics in this book is to blame your employees. It works, but the emotional pain associated with it isn't worth it to me.

Have you ever worked for a boss who does no wrong? If anything is screwed up in his organization, it's the fault of the people who work for him. In a way, it's true, but who is responsible for directing the activities of these people? For a person to hold himself harmless from the activities of his employees tells me the person lacks loyalty and should be avoided.

Zapping your employees is easy. Your employees have no defense. They did screw up, and if you don't defend them then no one else will. Management wants to punish someone for failure, and they will accept one of your people if you are willing to offer her up. They don't care who—the system simply demands that *someone* be punished.

The most blatant use of this tactic is to say when asked why there was a failure, "I told him to do it, and he didn't." That statement may be true or not; it doesn't matter. Management will believe you because you're the manager. Employees are known to lie to protect themselves—Master Corporate Politicians don't lie, right? When you use this version of the tactic, you're signing the employee's death warrant. He's headed for the grinder, and you can no longer count on him in any future organizational plans.

An offshoot of this tactic is not to blame your employees but, when they're persecuted, not to defend them either. It works like this:

Boss: Your organization really screwed up. What happened?

You: I assigned this one to Jones. He tried real hard, but _____ didn't support him, and he failed.

Boss: So, Jones didn't cut the mustard?

You: No, Sir, but he tried. If _____ had done as expected, then Jones would've done it.

Boss: Looks to me like you need to find another job for Jones. I'm not sure we can trust him with something so critical again.

Is Jones dead? Maybe, and most likely. Were you at fault? You bet! You should have monitored Jones's performance and assured his success, or have been a party to his failure. Maybe you did, and were, but there may be times when you need your subordinates to take a fall for you. To sacrifice an employee every time you fail as a manager will yield you a staff of people who will not take any chances and rely completely on you and your ability. At some point in time you won't be able to use this tactic and there may be a time you really need it. Use it sparingly.

I once worked for a man who didn't know anything about material management. He was a good people manager, knew corporate politics, and made tough decisions—a real dynamic guy. He hired me to take the fall for him until he could get things fixed. I didn't realize it until I was dead, but I watched him work and have to say that today I admire him. He tried to protect me until one of his mistakes was critical. After taking the blame for three or four real blunders, I was a *persona non grata*. He did take care of me as best he could, but I was the official scapegoat. Using me, he rose from midlevel management to vice president. I followed him up the ladder until I was so cut up from taking the blame that he couldn't promote me.

Another offshoot is to let the boss blame the employee and for you to defend him and accept the blame. You do this after you're sure the boss is convinced the employee was the responsible party and will not let you accept the responsibility. The tactic plays out like this:

You: I should have monitored him more closely. If I had watched him and counseled him more closely, then it wouldn't have happened.

Boss: I won't accept that. You have too many employees to watch every action they make. He should have known better, and as far as I'm concerned, he screwed it up all by himself.

You: I feel responsible. I should have done a better job of managing him.

Boss: You're a good manager. You can't help it if you have crummy employees.

What did you accomplish in this exchange? You let the boss know you were willing to take the fall, and you let him think you were a good manager who was willing to protect his employees. If you must use the this tactic, this version is preferable.

Using other people to take the blame for your failures has its liabilities. The person you stuck the blame on will remember you did it, and the relationship will never be the same—you'll kill the drive in a self-motivated individual.

This is a tactic of last resort. Don't use it unless you have no other alternatives.

Blame Procurement

In short, Luck's always to blame.
JEAN DE LA FONTAINE (1621–95)

An old and very cagey production manager once told me after I had given notice and was leaving the company, "If procurement didn't exist, I would have to invent it. The best excuse a manufacturing manager could ever ask for." What did he mean? He meant he could blame all his failures on the buyers. When I worked with him, he did exactly that. He was never at fault, but I and my procurement organization were always screwing up and responsible for him not meeting the master production schedule. Was he right in blaming me? No, but that's corporate politics. He was a mediocre manager who knew his politics, and every failure was the fault of procurement. If he had two hundred total shortages, the three held for purchased material were holding up the other one hundred and ninety-seven. Not true, but he had the senior management convinced.

The message in this section is if you're a production manager, think of how you can blame all of your problems on the buyers. They're always late in deliveries, right? If those lazy loafers would get off their butts and bring in your parts, then you could meet schedule, right? The fact that you can't find skilled machinists to take the parts and finish them, and the fact that you have no production control system to manage your priorities—well, those just aren't the issues.

There are a million reasons why a production line can't meet schedule, but the one that's not under your control is procurement. If all the blame for your failures is focused on them, then your own failures are hidden. Think about it.

If you're an engineer, then procurement is holding you up for some parts you need to make your prototype. If you're quality control then the buyers are sitting on a buy for some equipment that would allow you to reduce manufacturing failures by catching it at receiving inspection. If you're production control and had all your purchased parts, you could schedule production to run more efficiently.

Keep in mind you can make similar statements about virtually every organization. Procurement is particularly vulnerable because they're at the tail end of a long series of events that must happen before a smooth running production line can occur. If the bills of material are no good, if the engineering is no good, if the master schedule is no good, and if the suppliers fall behind schedule, then the whole process collapses and the buyers get the blame. They're an easy target and are always vulnerable.

Remember, *"If procurement didn't exist, I would have to invent it."*

Blame Data Processing

No science is immune to the infection of politics and the corruption of power.

JACOB BRONOWSKI (1908–74)

Many people dislike data-processing people—they're often arrogant and self-important. They can't do what you want, and when they do, it costs you a fortune. As a Master Corporate Politician trainee, does this sound like an area to dump problems? If you said yes, you're catching on.

The shifting of focus is key to your success. If you can keep your accuser's attention diverted to something other than your failure, you may gain enough time to fix the problem. Data-processing people, like doctors, lend themselves to attack. Have you ever wondered why doctors get sued so often? Well, I think it's because they're often arrogant and charge you ten times what their services are worth. When they make a mistake, and everyone does, the patient gets so angry he almost feels as if it's necessary for punishment to take place. It's the same with data-processing people.

Think about it. How many computer-related problems do you have? What happens when you call them? They tell you it will take six months and cost a zillion dollars. When they finally get around to giving it (the fix) to you, it doesn't work the way you wanted. When they finally get that fixed, the data is no good, so your reports are useless. When they add the edit routines to clean up the data, the computer goes down. Blame it on data processing? Yes, it's easy. Here are a few examples that work for me:

- Why no reports? The computer went down.

- Why is the data no good? Data processing didn't put in any edit routines.

- Why is the report useless? Data processing has a program error.

- Why can't I get my job done? It's going to take them a year to give me the computer report I need. I can't do my job effectively until then.

- Why am I over budget? The cost of data processing blew the hell out of the budget. A hundred thousand dollars a year for this garbage? Can't anybody control those guys?

- Why doesn't anybody like the system? Data processing picked this system, and it doesn't work.

- When is somebody going to fix the system so we can get reports that will allow us to manage our business? Never, we can't afford those guys.

- Why didn't I respond? If I had some notice out of the computer—a warning of my problem—then I could have taken corrective action.

- Why won't it work? The damned thing is so complicated nobody in my department can use it.

- Why isn't the work getting done? I get forty pounds of paper a day from those idiots, and not a single page is usable. I need a summary report—I can't manage without one.

- Why is the program still not working? Fifty thousand dollars! All I wanted was a simple little change.

Another reason I like to blame data processing is because these guys never get fired. You can dump on them all day long, and they still manage to survive. Why? I don't know—I don't really understand their magic. Sometimes I wish I had their nine lives. I've had some of my most bitter fights with them, catching them in the act of screwing up, and they seem to survive. You can't get a data-processing guy—they just won't die. An immortal breed.

Other Higher Priorities

Divine right of kings means the divine right of anyone who can get uppermost.
HERBERT SPENCER (1820–1903)

Have you ever noticed that almost all executives and professionals have staff to control the people who are waiting to see them? Doctors have receptionists, executives have secretaries, and even the grocery stores have a system of controlling you while you wait. Waiting is a way of life, and this section is going to show you a way of cutting the waiting time, or jumping to the head of the line.

Everybody responds to priorities. As a Master Corporate Politician, one of your jobs will be to balance priorities. Everybody wants his stuff first. "Take care of me now, and the others later." No one wants to wait, and if your career is riding on the successful completion of a project or assignment, you can't afford to wait.

In the movie *The Blues Brothers*, the two main characters said they were on a mission from God. There isn't a higher priority than that, is there? As a Master Corporate Politician, what's the highest priority you can think of? A directive from the CEO? The minutes of the board meeting? As you're thinking of items that would be considered priorities, why not make a list of everything that would get first-class treatment in your organization.

Make a list, and then rank them from high to low. Mine looks something like this:

1. Directive from the chairman/president

2. Directive from the vice president and general manager

3. Directive from the vice president of operations

4. Directive from my boss's boss

5. Directive from another vice president

6. A safety or security violation

7. A directive from the vice president and program manager

8. Directives from the other program managers

9. An edict from contracts

10. An edict from quality assurance

The list could go on forever until we reached the level where whatever it was we were talking about had no priority at all. How do you use this list? If you need priority, you need to see to it that you have one of the directives or edicts with you at all times. Are they hard to get? No, in fact they're quite easy.

Let me give you a few examples. You need your parts pushed through the receiving dock faster than the normal two-year cycle that it takes. How do you get it done? You could go down there and beg like the rest of the people who are waiting for their stuff, or you can go to the vice president of material and tell him if your parts don't get through today, then the production line will be going down and the general manager will be looking for heads. What happens? You'll get your parts.

Let's say you want one of your jobs moved on the factory floor faster than normal because you promised a customer two-week delivery to get the sale. You need the sale because your salary is based on it, and you know it normally takes the factory six to eight weeks to manufacture that part. After trying the production control manager and being told he won't be able to ship until next July, ten to twelve weeks from now, you're desperate. What do you do? You go find a vice president, the one responsible for sales and marketing if you can.

Why a marketing guy? Marketing vice presidents always get what they want, when they want it. Look at your company. I bet you'll find it's the same way there—it generally is everywhere. Marketing guys carry clout because if they don't bring in the sales, nobody eats. When you get to this guy—there's a line at his door too—you explain the importance of your sale and the prospects of follow-on business if the company delivers as promised. You'll probably get his help.

Does jerking the system around to get other than normal priorities hurt a company? You bet! When you blow something through ahead of normal, the other stuff waits and becomes late. Once it's late, it has to be blown through, creating other late stuff. The vicious cycle begins, and the only way you can get anything is with priority. Nothing is routine; everything is late.

Should this concern you? Yes, but as a Master Corporate Politician you live by one motto. Clint Eastwood had a line for this one too, "A man's got to do what a man's got to do." If you can't get what you need, when you need it, then screw the system and get help.

How can you as a Master Corporate Politician use this as a defense? You can claim that the general manager screwed up your production line causing you to miss this month's schedule. Will it save your butt when they start the inquisition? Nope, you're going to be ground , but as they dip you down into the grinder, you can scream out it wasn't your fault. As the executioner molds your once-firm flesh into a semisolid patty, he'll yell back at you that you should have planned for that.

The message? Grab all of these kinds of excuses you can. Every time someone jerks off your schedule or puts you into an abnormal mode, record it. One excuse isn't enough to save you from the grinder, but if you have a wheelbarrow full of them, it might. Resist any attempt to override your normal priority scheme, and when they do it to you, record it.

Summary

If you remember that the Master Corporate Politicians are all out there just waiting for you to screw up so they can eat you, this chapter could save your life. Reasons for failure that don't affix the failure to you are important. Such things as never admitting failure, using honesty, shifting focus, blaming others, and other priorities are very useful in avoiding the grinder.

chapter 8

Secure a Safe Place on the Food Chain

In this chapter, we'll discuss the methods of really fixing a failure. The previous chapters dealt with how to avoid doing this, or effectively putting it off. I'll show you some methods Master Corporate Politicians use to fix failures. They use trial balloons, go right to the top, personal attacks, and name-dropping. We will also discuss firing people and resumes and hiring. I'll show you how to effectively take over an organization and give you some thoughts on risk. Last, I'll give you a technique used by many Master Corporate Politicians to get a dirty job done without risking themselves.

Trial Balloons

> When a thing ceases to be a subject of controversy, it
> ceases to be a subject of interest.
>
> **WILLIAM HAZLITT** (1778–1830)

Have you ever seen a low-level government bureaucrat make a statement on the evening news about policy and then watch his bosses, the higher-ups, disclaim his remarks the next night if the public reaction was unfavorable? If favorable, the higher-ups implement it and take the credit. Master Corporate Politicians do the same thing every day.

How does it work? Easy, let me give you an example.

The Situation: The manager of quality is inadvertently holding up shipments because parts can't get through receiving inspection. He has a high staff turnover and can't get enough inspectors to handle the volume. You don't want him mad at you because he can reject you out of business—reject every shipment that comes in. A quality guy once said to me, "Don't screw with me, Dude. There isn't a part made that I can't find something wrong with, if I wanted to." Your objective is to get the situation fixed without turning the quality manager into one of your enemies.

The Plan: You call in a loyal subordinate and ask her to come to a meeting with the general manager and the quality manager and to complain bitterly about the backlog. You want her to suggest that the receiving inspection task be "farmed out" to a local laboratory. If the general manager likes the idea, no sweat. If he doesn't, you'll step in and save the subordinate from the general manager's wrath and protect her from the quality manager's retribution. Regardless of what the general manager wants, you personally will not offend the quality manager.

The Execution: The subordinate does as requested, and the quality manager immediately jumps to the defensive. He claims the turnaround time has been reduced considerably and in thirty days things will be back to normal. He also claims because of staff shortages, he has had to work his existing staff overtime and he doesn't have any budget left to finance an off-load plan.

Outcome #1: If you sense, by watching the general manager's reactions to quality's arguments, that he's siding with or sympathetic to quality, then you might say, "My subordinate and I haven't talked about this serious problem. I'm satisfied quality's working the problem and will have it fixed soon. I recommend we give him some more time, because we can always off-load if we need to."

Outcome #2: If you sense the general manager's not swayed by quality's arguments and can't make up his mind, you might say, "This is a temporary problem that's causing us to miss production schedule. I suggest we off-load until Quality's caught up. Since I know he'll be caught up in thirty days, we would have to off-load for a only week or so, and it would guarantee us that we won't be shut down for parts. If it's a budget problem, I'll transfer a few bucks from my budget."

Outcome #3: If you sense the general manager's really pissed off at quality, then the wisest policy is to say nothing and let the general manager handle the situation any way he wants.

Let's analyze your words. In the first case, where the general manager didn't want to off-load, you appeared to side with quality over your own subordinate, but did you? You got your message across to the general manager without personally attacking quality. You let the general manager know you considered the problem serious, and that he needs to watch those guys closely.

You also made it clear that the issue wasn't closed until the backlog was gone. In the second case, where the general manager was wavering, you took a middle-of-the-road solution which was to off-load only until the backlog's gone. You gave the quality guy credit for fixing his problem with, "I know he'll be caught up," you effectively closed down any more arguments from quality by offering to pay for it, and you fixed your problem. In the last instance, where the general manager was angry with quality, you could have chosen any of several options:

- Pour salt into quality's wounds.

- Gently defend quality. You may need the IOU later.

- Keep your mouth shut and let the general manager eat the guy for lunch.

Using trial balloons allows you to distance yourself from a problem or controversy until you know which way the boss is headed. Once you know, then you can act with reasonable confidence that the boss is behind you. Very few senior-level corporate executives commit themselves to an action until they have run a few trial balloons.

Topside

For nothing can seem foul to those that win.

WILLIAM SHAKESPEARE (1564–1616)

Did you ever try to take something back to a department store only to have some surly clerk tell you it couldn't be returned? Angered, you went to the store manager and he graciously accepted the return. This is the way life is. If you want something, go right to the top. Why waste your time dealing with the subordinates? You know they don't have the power or authority to fix the problem, so why not go right to the top?

How does a Master Corporate Politician use this tactic? She uses it mostly as a threat to get what she wants, but she's not afraid to use it when it's called for. I personally like to give the subordinates a chance to do what they should be doing, but they're often lazy and uncaring, so I have to topside them. The Master Corporate Politician will never announce when she's going to do it, she'll just do it.

When used, the topside tactic is devastating. You go to the top person and tell him how his organization is not doing its job, screwing you, or generally not performing to spec, and he gets angry. He's not angry at you, but angry that he's having to fix something that should have been handled at a much lower level than his. The wrath of this guy will be enough to get his troops moving, and they'll be more careful the next time they deal with you.

The methods of topsiding a guy are many. You can do it in a casual conversation with the guy's boss, as in, "Oh, by the way," or you can do it with a formal protest. You can do it by writing a letter to the guy's boss and copy the boss's boss, or you can have your boss do it for you. Topside solutions almost always yield results. Here are some examples.

Sometimes you topside a person directly. I was having trouble with a contracts manager. He was quoting me the standard lead time on a part that his company produced, and the standard lead time wouldn't support my factory schedule. I called the president of his company, and I got my parts in half the normal lead time.

Sometimes you topside a person by having someone else apply pressure. A supplier of mine was having trouble getting paid by my accounts-payable department. The accounts-payable people were about a month behind, and all my suppliers were screaming. I told him to put me on credit hold and write a letter to the general manager saying that until he was paid in full, he wasn't shipping a damned thing. He was paid that week.

The Master Corporate Politician is not afraid to go to the top. It seems to motivate people. I use it all the time and have yet to have it backfire on me. If you can't get someone to do something that is reasonable, or is his job, go see his boss, or his boss's boss. If the whole organization is full of idiots, keep going up the ladder until you're at the top. If that fails, go to the newspapers and television stations. If you put enough pressure on a Master Corporate Politician, he'll do what you want.

Personal Attacks

> *There is no way to penetrate the surface of life but by attacking it earnestly at a particular point.*
> CHARLES HORTON COOLEY (1864–1929)

I love this tactic. It's so basic and so brutal. What is a personal attack? As the name implies, it's an attack on an individual with lies and untruths designed to make him angry and make mistakes. How does it work? Read on:

Me: You guys aren't doing your job, and it's affecting my job performance.

Other Guy: Well, we've had some problems.

Me: I don't want to hear about your problems. You and your whole department are incompetent.

Other Guy: I resent that. I'm not incompetent.

Me: You're the most incompetent idiot I know—useless! I don't know how you manage to stay employed. It must be because you're such a kiss-ass. It sure isn't because you're doing your job.

I could continue the dialogue, but you can see that I'm working him to anger. I want him to be angry because I know one of three things will happen. He'll direct that anger at the problem, he'll direct it at me, or he'll direct it at both the problem and at me. Most likely he'll fix the problem and he'll hate my guts, but he'll fix the problem. Nobody likes to be labeled an incompetent. If a few people start saying it, then a lot of people will say it. Even if it's not true, it will become accepted.

I got the most angry response in my career when I called a man a cocksucker. I told him that all he knew how to do was that, and if he didn't learn his job I was going to tell the whole world. I got his attention because he wasn't—I knew he wasn't—but he knew if I told everyone he was, he would be labeled one. Dirty? Yes. Did he do what I wanted? Of course.

Using personal attacks does two things for you. Generally, it gets the person's attention and gets him or her moving to fix the problem; second, it creates an enemy. I try not to use this tactic on peers, but it is relatively safe to use it on subordinates in another organization. I've never worried about making enemies of subordinates, because if you come back later and apologize, they're anxious to accept. They don't want you for an enemy because they know you can do more to hurt them than they can to hurt you.

This tactic is brutal and effective. When you've gotten your way and the failure is actually fixed, I recommend you do apologize and try to make friends. He'll be more careful the next time he fails to do what you want, and more responsive to your requests for corrective action.

Name-Dropping

> *In real life, unlike in Shakespeare, the sweetness of the rose depends upon the name it bears. Things are not only what they are. They are, in very important respects, what they seem to be.*
>
> HUBERT H. HUMPHREY (1911–78)

A cousin to the RULE #1, *It's who you know* (see page 2) is this tactic—name dropping. Do you hate name-droppers? I do. I hate their guts, but I've learned that when you need to get something fixed, it helps to have a strong ally whose name you can use to get people moving.

How does a Master Corporate Politician use the name-dropping tactic? He uses it subtly, but with such iron-glove finesse that the hearer knows that unless she responds, the wrath of the gods will fall on her head. Such statements as, "The chairman wants such and such to happen" are typical of the Master Corporate Politician's use of the tactic. Another use might be, "The general manager's really going to be pissed if this doesn't happen."

Does name-dropping help? Yes, particularly if the hearer knows you really do have the person's ear. If she thinks you're bluffing or bullshitting, it will backfire on you and could be more trouble than it was worth.

Do I use name-dropping? Very rarely. I use the tactic to gain the person's ear, but I never mention it to win an argument. Others know I do, when I do, and that's usually enough. Should you use name-dropping? By all means. If you have the attention of a powerful person, as a Master Corporate Politician you should use it.

Being able to drop a name or two successfully is almost as good as being the person's son. It's amazing to me to watch someone seize power when he or she is friends with the big boss. Everyone will go out of their way not to offend the name-dropper.

There was a movie I saw a long time ago that starred Frank Sinatra. Frank was Johnny Concho, and his brother was Red Concho. Red was a feared gunfighter, and Johnny used his brother's name and influence to push the townspeople around. When his brother was killed, Johnny got pushed around himself. Use the name-dropping tactic with care. When your man dies, you will too.

Firing People

You have sat too long for any good you have been doing. Depart, I say, and let us have done with you. In the name of God, go!

OLIVER CROMWELL (1599–1658)

How do you fire someone? With a lot of pain. It's not easy on either side of the table. Being fired is tough, but firing people is almost as hard—you know you're screwing up a person's life forever. Regardless of what else happens to them, they will always remember the day you fired them. They look at you with eyes that beg you to say it's a joke, but the eyes also tell you they know it's real and there's nothing either of you can do to stop it.

How do I do it? I come right to the point and tell the person. I say, "You're being terminated for _____." I don't say anything else, but rather wait until the employee says something. When he does, and he will, respond directly to the statement. If you've done a good job as a manager, the termination shouldn't be a surprise to the employee. You should have had several counseling sessions with him already, letting him know something he was doing wasn't considered satisfactory.

Is it easy? Nope, never has been. I've fired maybe a dozen people in my career. It's tough even when you've told the employee many times to correct the problem or face termination. It's tough, period.

Do it cleanly, but do it. If a person needs termination, or deserves it, you have to do it. If you don't, you're sending a message to the rest of your employees that the behavior of that employee will be tolerated. If you accept it in one person, then you'll accept it from all. Make your decision, and execute it.

Are you going to suffer as a result of doing it? If you're human you will, but if you don't do it, the suffering you endure will be far greater. You have to do it—your career may depend on firing a nonperforming employee.

How do I do it? I get mad at the employee. I've told him many times his behavior was unsatisfactory—I've warned him and tried to get him to change, but he didn't. It's almost as if he's asking me to fire him. I get angry at him and at myself. We've both failed, but he has to pay the price.

Firing people is tough on everyone involved, but it's an action the employee has asked you to do, so do it!

Resumés and Hiring

When I give a man an office, I watch him carefully to see whether he is swelling or growing.
WOODROW WILSON (1856–1924)

I don't know any more about hiring people than you do. It's almost like getting married. You don't know what you have until it's too late. Once the ring is on, you're committed, and once he starts work, you own him. What do you do to weed out the losers? That's what this section is all about.

The first step in the hiring process is the resume. I hate resumes, but that's the way the system is. Resumés are good for only one purpose—getting you an interview. A resume should be used as a sales tool to get you in the door. It should sell you. If it doesn't sell you, it needs to be rewritten.

What's good in a resume, and what's bad? I don't like resumes that just tell about accomplishments and ignore the positions held and responsibilities. Accomplishments don't mean anything to me because I don't know what level the individual was when he did it. Was he part of a team that did it? Was he the team leader? Was he just a flunky who did what he was told and is now trying to claim credit for its success? Tell me what positions you held, what your responsibilities were, and then tell me what your accomplishments were. I need all three. If you just send me a resume that tells me what your accomplishments were, I'll never call you in for an interview.

When looking for supervisors, I want to know that the person has supervised before. If your current management won't give you a chance as a supervisor, why should I? I don't take risks unless I have to, and I'm surely not going to risk screwing up my organization by hiring an untested supervisor.

I like formal education. I have lots of it, and I look for it in people I'm hiring. It tells me the guy was willing to pay the price—education is basically just putting in the time. In some cases, you don't learn a heck of a lot, but just by having the paper—the sheepskin—you show you were willing to put up with the educational system. It says a lot to me.

I like experience too, and I try to hire people who know more than I do. If I could pick a perfect staff, it would consist of people who were all about fifty-five to sixty years old who still had some guts left. Experience is the best teacher, and I like to hire people who have been there and can help me get there. If you have experience, list it. Most Master Corporate Politicians want veterans, not rookies.

If you have a college degree, I don't care that you graduated from high school. You had to graduate to get into college. If you're trying to get a job in accounting, no one cares that you flipped burgers at Burger King. I want to know how well you know accounting and how well you think.

Should you use a resume service? Perhaps, as long as you pay attention to what I've already said. List your experience and your education and make sure the resume tells how you'll fit into my organization. That is what will sell you.

Do I, or anyone else, care what your career objective is? Not really. I want you to help me fulfill *my* objectives. If I hire you, your objectives better be my objectives, or you won't last long. Don't list it on the resume. It's a waste of space.

What does this whole section have to do with actually fixing failures? Hiring people is the key to fixing anything. People do the work, and finding people who can do it is tough. I've already told you what I look for in a resume, and you should consider similar criteria. People fix problems, and hiring the good ones is like selecting a marriage partner. Be careful.

Hard at First, Ease Up Later

A man may be a tough, concentrated, successful money-maker and never contribute to his country anything more than a horrible example. A manager may be tough and practical, squeezing out, while the going is good, the last ounce of profit and dividend, and may leave behind him an exhausted industry and a legacy of industrial hatred. A tough manager may never look outside his own factory walls or be conscious of his partnership in a wider world. I often wonder what strange cud such men sit chewing when their working days are over, and the accumulating riches of the mind have eluded them.

ROBERT MENZIES (1894–1978)

I should call this the military-commander tactic because nearly every one of them uses it. Why? Because it works. I spent almost three years in the army and every commanding officer I served under used it.

What is it? When you take command of an outfit, or an organization, you have several methods of introducing yourself. You can be quiet for a while and learn what is going on, or you can do what the military teaches its officers to do. Commanding officers assume the previous commander didn't know a thing about running an outfit, and they also assume everyone who works for them is incompetent until proven otherwise. If you think that way, how are you going to approach the organization? You're going to hit it as if you were John Wayne, Rambo, and Clint Eastwood all rolled up in one—you're going to kick ass and take names, right? If I thought that way, I would.

Despite my military officer training, I don't think that way. I assume everyone who works for me is competent, and the previous administrator knew what he was doing but he ran into problems he couldn't solve. However, I don't let anyone know that, and I act as if I were the stereotypical army officer. I scream and yell and threaten. You should watch the staff fly off to carry out my commands—like rats scurrying around a room. Why do I do this? Because it's necessary. I've established an understanding that if I don't get my way, I become a monster. Once I've established that I have a monster inside of me, then I can act normal and treat people as human beings.

Why go through the charade of being tough, if you aren't? Remember the old Western story of the gunfighter who had arthritis so bad he couldn't move his fingers—he had to have his wife dress him every morning? He was still feared ten years after the last time he drew his gun. The same logic applies to management.

Why were you given the job? Was it because the last guy couldn't get it done? Was it because the last guy didn't have the horsepower, or political clout, to make it happen? If so, then you need an organization that is a little bit afraid of you. You don't want them terrorized, but you do want them to be midair and asking how high when you yell "jump." Why? You want it because if you have it, then you never have to worry about getting people to do what you want. Like the aging gunfighter, your reputation will be enough and you'll never have to draw your gun again.

Use this tactic the next time you take over an organization. Once you've been acerbic for a while, you can return to being a nice guy and people will forgive you. They're sitting out there right now begging for the chance to forgive you. Don't worry about it. Do what you have to do. They will forgive you.

No Guts, No Glory

You take a number of small steps which you believe are right, thinking maybe tomorrow somebody will treat this as a dangerous provocation. And then you wait. If there is no reaction, you take another step: courage is only an accumulation of small steps.

GEORGE KONRÁD (b. 1933)

Another military saying? If you haven't figured it out by now, the army had a pronounced effect on me and my thinking. I love the expression, NO GUTS, NO GLORY. It sums up life so well that I think it can be applied to just about any situation. The term "guts" can have several meanings, depending on the context. Guts can mean your willingness to work to get what you want. It can mean your ability to take risk. It may mean your ability to withstand pain to get what you want. Define it as you see fit, and if you don't already, you'll start liking the saying too.

Suppose guts means willingness to work. I see a lot of young people today who want to be chairman of the board, but are unwilling to pay the price. They want it, but they don't have the guts to get there. They're unwilling to go to night school, work the extra hours, come in on weekends, or do anything else extraordinary to get it. They want it handed to them. How do you communicate the concept of guts to young people? How do you communicate it to your staff?

I asked a friend of mine why no one ever picked a fight with me—I saw organizational fights all over the place, but none involving me. My friend told me that they didn't fight with me because I had a reputation of not letting go until I won. I was known as a bulldog that puts his teeth into something and doesn't let go until it dies. Are you that way? Should you be? Think of the aging gunfighter. His reputation did all the fighting for him. Do you like fights? I don't, and I don't like them so much that when I get in one, I fight to kill. I'm not one to wound you—if you mess with me, count on one of us dying.

Why was John Wayne so respected and well liked? Was it because he was such a good actor? Was it because he had such good scripts? No. It was because his roles stood for guts and determination. You didn't beat Old John. He was American and he was tough. John Wayne had guts.

Another aspect of guts is risk taking. Does it take guts to take a risk that may end your career? Does it take guts to quit your job and start your own business? Does it take guts to tell your boss that she is an idiot? Yes, to all the above. If you want something, then you have to be willing to take a risk to get it. Nobody is going to give it to you. You have to be willing to suffer to get what you want, or to get something fixed. Only the ones taking risks are getting anything done.

Most people agree that there are two kinds of people, mice and men. If you're a mouse, this tactic is probably very amusing to you. If you're a real man, or real woman, then you're wondering why I'm even writing about it—you know about it already and are wondering when I'm going to get to something else that you can use. I'm writing about it because there are a ton of people out there that haven't decided what they are. This section is attempting to persuade them to become a John Wayne or Carry Nation, not a Wally Cox or Herman Milktoast.

How badly do you want it fixed? If you aren't ready to endure pain and suffering, you must not want it fixed very badly. If you're not willing to risk it all, it must not be worth fighting for. If it isn't worth fighting for, why risk a career or your job? Sit back and let somebody else do it. If it gets bad enough, someone will come forward and fix it, right? Why stick your neck out and risk the possibility of getting killed? Let the other guy get decimated for the corporation, not you.

If you believe what I just said, throw this book away and plan on retiring in middle management, if you are lucky. Only the risk takers ever make it to the top. Look at the long-distance runners. Long-distance running takes guts. By the time you reach the third mile, your lungs hurt, your legs feel like lead, and your head's pounding. Are they taking a risk? Of course. They're risking that they won't finish, or that they'll injure themselves. Long-distance running is a lot like corporate politics—you have to keep doing it, even when it hurts, until you get to the finish line.

Each race, each encounter, is one more step toward getting to the top. Each time you fix a failure, you step one inch closer to the top. If you avoid the failure, or fail to run the race, then you've moved nowhere and perhaps have slid down a little.

Take a risk and run the race. When you do, don't stop running until you're finished, or you're pronounced dead. Don't quit until you look down at your body and see worms eating your dead carcass. When you see that, you'll know for sure that any additional effort would be useless. Don't let your legs, mind, guts, or desire stop until you've gotten what you want. If you stop, you'll wind up like most of middle management, redefining your objectives to match what you have. They quit, and when they did, told themselves that what they had was enough. As a friend of mine said about his romantic pursuits, "If you can't find a lover who meets your standards, lower your standards." If this is how you want to run your life, be my guest. If you want to win, have guts.

Reread this section often. If you're having trouble with anything, remember, "If you ain't got guts, then you ain't got nothing."

As Long as I Don't Know

All things truly wicked start from an innocence.
ERNEST HEMINGWAY (1899–1961)

Did you watch the Democrats work over Ollie North and Admiral Poindexter a few years ago? How about Clinton and the DNC campaign-funding disaster? I did, and it brought to mind this tactic, which I use occasionally. What did they say that made me think of it? They said the President didn't know what they were doing, but we—the TV viewers—all thought he did. What does that mean? It means he knew, but he didn't. Sound like corporate politics? He knew what they were doing, but they never told him, and therefore he could deny he knew.

Let me tell you how to use this tactic. If someone who works for you wants to do something that could lay you out on an ant field if it fails, simply refuse to authorize it. While saying they better not do it, you also say that if you don't know what's happening, you can't stop it.

Another army story. Let me tell you about basic training in the United States Army. I had a drill instructor—they called themselves drill sergeants—the toughest hombres God ever created. John Wayne was a wimp in comparison. We had some draftees who were deserting like roaches fleeing bug spray. He called a few of us together and told us not to punish the deserters—that it was against army regulations. He also told us if the problem didn't stop, the whole company was going to be punished. He told us some of the other companies had instituted a voluntary watch program, which ensured that people didn't desert. He also suggested that some of the other companies had beaten the shit out of the deserters. He told us that doing it was against the Uniform Code of Military Justice—he winked when he did. The next deserter the MPs brought back got the shit beaten out of him. We didn't have any more desertions.

What did the drill sergeant do? He used corporate politics. He told us not to do it, but he graphically told us how to. We followed his instructions. Are your people the way we were? I think so. I use this tactic all the time. I just say, "You know what your job is. If you need to do something you know is wrong but will help the materials department, as long as I don't know you're breaking the rules, do what you have to." I also let them know that if they get caught breaking the rules, I'll punish them. I've only had to punish one guy in over thirty years, and I rewarded him afterwards.

Do what you have to—you have to get the job done, and sometimes it means being a Master Corporate Politician. Do what you have to, to win. If you don't, the other guy will, and you'll wind up working for him.

Summary

There are many ways of actually fixing a failure. I have related a few of the more successful methods I have used to help me. We talked about how to introduce a potentially unpopular idea—the trial balloon. We talked of going right to the top of an organization, using personal attacks and name-dropping. We went over the basics of firing people and hiring their replacements. I've shown you how some people take over an organization, and I discussed a philosophy on risk. We also talked about how to let your subordinates do what needs doing without your involvement.

There is a time in a Master Corporate Politician's life when he or she actually has to fix something. When you've run out of tactics and are forced to perform, then reread this chapter and go do it.

chapter **9**

Keeping the Pack in Line

There are many ways to manage and develop your subordinates. I've selected a few of the most significant ones for this chapter. If you plan on staying with a company very long, developing your people will be one of the most vital keys to your success. In this chapter, we will cover loyalty—my version of it. I'll show you how to handle ambitious employees and how to set up a pretty good staff just by taking people whom everyone else has deemed losers. I'll show you how one of my ex-bosses handled an eager beaver intent on eating our lunches, and I'll give you a tip on expanding something good in your life to the point it gets you or one of your employees a promotion. I'll reveal one of my most effective methods of getting more effort out of my subordinates, and I'll show you how important it is to keep your employees in sight of your management. I'll tell you how to shame an employee into doing more, and I'll talk about how important it is to have an esprit de corps.

Loyalty Up & Down

We are all the President's men.

HENRY KISSINGER (b. 1923)

Loyalty to those below you can be rewarded long after the time they work for you. Over ten years ago, when I first joined a large aerospace company, I saw this principle in action. It's just as true today.

"What does that guy do for a living," I quietly asked a friend of mine, referring to an older man from our department who didn't seem to do anything. He rarely showed up for work, and when he did, I couldn't see that he did anything. He smelled of alcohol almost every day, and one day I saw him sleeping at his desk at ten o'clock in the morning.

"Anything he wants," responded my friend, who had been with the company many years.

"Is it a discipline problem?" I asked.

"No, he does whatever you tell him to do. He just doesn't do it very well, so no one ever asks him to do anything."

"Why don't they fire him?" I asked.

"The old man used to be the department manager. A very powerful manager, too. He's the one that recognized our vice president's potential when the vice president was just an hourly wage earner. That old man there sponsored the vice president and helped him get started up the ladder. The vice president won't let anyone fire him." You may be sponsoring future vice presidents or people who can get you a job when this one falls apart—treat your people fairly.

Is that loyalty, or what? The vice president remembered, and this old alcoholic still had a job. I remember this every time I think of the word "loyalty." If you keep a wino on the payroll and defend his existence against anyone, that's loyalty. If you take care of your people, when you later decide life's too tough and you want to become a muscatel guzzler, you may have a home too.

Ambitious Employees

Ambition can creep as well as soar.
EDMUND BURKE (1729–97)

Employees typically don't see themselves in the same perspective management does. An old saying in industry sums this up quite nicely:

If you could buy a man for what he's worth and sell him for what he thinks he's worth, you would be rich if you only had one man.

How does a manager cope with this when an employee is ambitious beyond his ability? My answer, by evasion.

Employee: I want that supervisor's job that just opened up.

Evasive Manager: Okay, I'll see to it that you're one of the candidates considered.

Notice how the manager handled the situation. First, he didn't tell the employee he already had a candidate picked out, and it wasn't he. Second, he didn't tell the man he wasn't worth a darn and there was absolutely no possibility he would even consider him. Third, the manager made the man no promises, other than to consider him.

How do you handle the situation when you select another, and your employee comes to you and wants to know why? I always recommend honesty—tactful honesty. Tell the employee the truth and what he can do to improve himself to be ready the next time an opportunity comes, but explain the facts. Just fixing his problems doesn't guarantee him a position—it's a combination of real ability, perceived ability, and opportunity. Want to see this in action? I refer you to the section called Corporate Politician's Image on page 11. It relates to a situation that happened to me when I asked why I did not get a position that had opened up.

Pick the Boneyard

Let us not be too particular. It is better to have old second-hand diamonds than none at all.

MARK TWAIN (1835–1910)

Several of my most successful organizations were built from boneyards. I did it selectively, but there are a ton of people who have been labeled losers who are out there waiting for their second chance. A wise Master Corporate Politician won't accept the judgment of the organization, but will make her own assessment. A second chance for a loser will give you a loyal employee. If he fails a second time, there will be no third. Most intelligent people know that. I love them, if they're competent.

Boneyards are resting places for all sorts of people. Many times, they're filled with political refugees. These are the guys who don't get along with management, or who were moved there so management could bring in one of their buddies from the last place they worked. If you hire a refugee, you need to be sure it's politically acceptable to do so. If management wants him dead, but can't fire him, it would be unwise to give him a productive job.

Time heals all wounds. It's a trite expression, but has some validity. After resting in the boneyard for a year or so, the pain or problem that caused management to put a person there will have dimmed and it may be possible to resurrect her. Is it likely? Not many managers will pick from the boneyard because of their fear that whoever put the person there will also put them there, or because they think the boneyard is full of people with a track record of failure. Refugees have hope in that people do quit or retire, and it's possible to find resurrection. Losers are losers and have no hope.

How do you know if you've been shuttled to the boneyard? Your title is the first indication. If it's special projects or some other nonspecific title, you may be there. How do you get out? You have to work your butt off, and wait. You've pissed someone off, and until you've served your time, you aren't going anywhere. Have I been in the boneyard? Yes, and I found another job—I was in a hurry to get to the top and wasn't about to spend a year or so waiting for management to forgive me.

A wise Master Corporate Politician keeps his eyes on the boneyards, and when he sees a good person stuck there, he works his tactics to get that person assigned to his department. Good people are hard to get, and if you can latch onto one from the boneyard, do it.

Other's Subordinates

Be nice to people on your way up because you'll meet them on your way down.

WILSON MIZNER (1876–1933)

I saw this tactic work and I couldn't believe it! My boss and I were having a lot of trouble with an eager beaver from accounting—he was eating us alive. He wasn't particularly smart, but he was dangerous—he would find data that looked as if our department was screwing up, and he would broadcast it to the world. We would explain it, but as I point out later, it can destroy you.

After the third time he did this, my boss called me and Eager Beaver into his office and chewed out Eager Beaver. My boss could take large hunks of your buttocks when he wanted to, and when he finished with the accountant, that guy didn't have any left. The next day, he did it again, and again on the following day. My boss's objective? I think it was to intimidate the accountant to the point that the man would leave us alone and go to greener pastures.

Did it work? Yes, and no. Eager Beaver went to his boss, the Controller, and complained he was being abused. The controller spoke to my boss, who did nothing but praise Eager Beaver and even asked the controller to let him hire the man. He said Eager Beaver was the best damned accountant he had ever worked with and the controller should be thankful the man was on his team. My boss praised him over and over, and then mentioned the problem he was having, but he acted surprised the accountant was so sensitive about their discussions of it. The controller couldn't very well complain to the general manager about my boss, because my boss had nothing but praise for Eager Beaver. I guess the controller told Eager Beaver to try a little harder to get along, because we didn't have any more trouble with him after that.

What was this tactic? The tactic was that when you need to tear apart another man's subordinate, do it, and if you're called up short for it, then praise the man as if he walked on water. Be sure the problem you're having with the subordinate is mentioned, but it's only a minor problem. It *must* be presented as a minor problem, even if it's the most serious problem you've ever encountered.

If a Little Is Good, More Is Better

I don't say 'tis impossible for an impudent man not to rise in the world, but a moderate merit with a large share of impudence is more probable to be advanced than the greatest qualifications without it.

LADY MARY WORTLEY MONTAGU (1689–1762)

This section might also have been included in Chapter 10 because you can use it to further your own career as well as your subordinates' careers. So what does it mean? If you reward a certain type of behavior, you're sure to see that type of behavior again. Think about it as it pertains to your non-corporate life. If your child is rewarded by your smiles and affection for something, she'll repeat it. B. F. Skinner, the noted behavioral psychologist, made a whole career writing about this phenomenon.

How is this applicable to furthering your subordinates' careers? You reward them for the behavior traits you like and ignore the ones you don't. Will it work? You bet it will, but it may take longer than just chewing their butt. And it will stay with them longer than a simple ass chewing for the undesirable behavior.

Now that you know how to use this principle as a management technique, think about how you can use it as a Master Corporate Politician would. Consider what these three examples have in common.

At my insistence, a friend of mine instituted a Statistical Process Control (SPC) training program to help my suppliers improve their quality and lower their costs. He did this and then started blowing his own horn about how much money he had saved the corporation. A few people listened and then a few more. In a few months, he was doing SPC training for the whole corporation. He expanded the SPC training into a whole new system that included a supplier-rating system and a complete new corporate organization that was in charge of implementing the new system. It made him a director, increased the cost of the product, and did little to improve supplier cost.

When the engineering problems on a particular subsystem became enormous, an engineer was brought into procurement to take charge of the subcontract. The engineer fixed the problem and suggested that if we had more engineers running things instead of the "narrow-minded subcontract administrators," we would save tons of money. He parlayed that idea into a directorship for himself that had all procurement reporting to the engineers who reported to him. This system has yet to yield any tangible results other than increased cost. It was a good idea on a limited scale, but stupid on a large one.

I was assigned to support a systems-implementation team that was getting in the way of real work. I needed to get them out of my work area so my people could get their work done. How did I do it? I suggested the team needed to be together and offered them the floor space in my organization. The team leader, an idiot, liked the idea and promptly moved his team into my area, almost causing a mutiny among my supervisors. I next suggested to the team leader that he needed his own building so he and his team could think and plan without all the interruptions caused by my noisy people. Once again, he liked it. Soon, he was gone, and the interruptions to my department diminished to the point we were no longer aware the team even existed. A little bit is good, and a whole lot is better.

The tendency of management is to accept the hypothesis that if something works on a limited scale, then it'll work much better on a larger one. They believe a person who's a winner on a small scale will be one on a larger scale. Their training and experience tells them this is the case. If you receive rewards for something you did on a small scale, consider enlarging it and see if you don't get more rewards. It doesn't matter if you know it won't work. Try it anyway.

The objective is to get management to say, "Good boy," and pat you on the head, right?

Try Just a Little Harder

The real leader has no need to lead—he is content to point the way.

HENRY MILLER (1891–1980)

Remember when you took your examinations in high school or college? When you finished, you told yourself that if you had studied just a little harder, you would have aced the exam? Remember running a race and when you lost by inches, saying to yourself that if you had run just a little harder, you could have won?

All people say to themselves that if they had studied a little harder or put forth a little more effort, they would have won. Effort is the only thing that separates winners from losers. People know this and a Master Corporate Politician can use it against them.

When a subordinate comes in and tells you he isn't going to finish a project on time, Fireproofing you (see page 71), what do you do? He wants Priority Control (see page 74) and says it can't all be done. What do you do? You use this tactic. Here's how it works:

Subordinate: I can't get all this work done—I need help.

Politician: What kind of help?

Subordinate: Anything! I can't get it all done. I'm really in trouble.

Politician: I don't think you're giving me all you have, are you? (You know the guy's working hard and needs help, but you can't give it to him. Besides, you would like to see him work a little harder.)

Subordinate: I'm working my ass off. Isn't that enough? (Notice his attempt to shift focus.)

Politician: You didn't answer my question. Are you giving me one hundred percent? I don't think so. I see you on the phone a lot, and I see you chewing the fat with the guys more than I think is necessary. Do you really think you're giving me one hundred percent?

Subordinate: I could do more, I guess, but I'm working my butt off, and I need some help. I work harder than anyone else in your department. (He does, but what difference does that make?)

Politician: I'll take care of them at salary review time. Do you think it's reasonable for me to help you when you're not giving me everything you have? I don't.

Subordinate: I'll keep trying, and I'll give you the one hundred percent you want.

What did the Master Corporate Politician do? He made the subordinate acknowledge the failure was due to the fact he wasn't trying hard enough. All people feel as if like failure is their fault even if only a small portion of the blame is theirs. If only they had tried harder!

When someone asks for a promotion or salary increase, what does the wise Master Corporate Politician do? She uses this tactic. "Do you think I should give you an increase when you're not giving me everything you have?" What about when the person asks you for a vacation, or to leave early for personal reasons. This tactic is dynamite and will add to the guilt feelings everyone has. Give an employee enough guilt, and he won't ask you for anything, ever!

Out of Sight, Out of Mind

Make visible what, without you, might perhaps never have been seen.

ROBERT BRESSON (b. 1907)

A saying in baseball, "They can't hit 'em if they can't see 'em," is true in corporate politics. You can't do anything with an employee if your management can't see him or her. I refuse to promote my own people when I don't personally know of their performance and activities. It's human nature. Would you promote one of your people if you didn't think he or she was any good? Even when your supervisors tell you the person's great—they jump buildings in a single bound—you should be reluctant to do anything with that employee unless you have some first hand knowledge about him.

Why? Every promotion or salary increase undergoes the scrutiny of higher management. Can you support this? Why are you promoting this guy, and not that one? What's he done that's so extraordinary? If you've ever gone into management and asked for money or a promotion for one of your people and couldn't defend your decision, you will understand. People have to make an impression at least one level above their immediate supervision to go anywhere. By the way, so do you!

What does a Master Corporate Politician do to overcome this situation? She goes on a campaign to advertise her superstars. Being a Master Corporate Politician means the Master Corporate Politician takes all the credit and none of the blame. This translates to none of the Master Corporate Politician's people ever getting any credit for good deeds, only blame for the failures. The Master Corporate Politician must overcome her natural tendency to suck up all the credit and let some of it flow to the selected subordinate. Here's how a good Master Corporate Politician does it:

Boss: You did a great job on that last project. It saved us millions of dollars. Thanks.

Corporate Politician: Thanks, Boss, but I couldn't have done it without my staff. They did most of the work. I was just the team leader. (Notice that the Master Corporate Politician never directly accepts credit, but she never denies it.)

Boss: What a team you assembled to do that task. That shows me quite a bit of leadership.

Corporate Politician: One man in particular was instrumental in the success of the project. If it hadn't been for _____, then the whole thing would've failed. If you get some time, it would mean a lot to him if you stopped by and let him know you know what an outstanding job he did.

Boss: Glad to.

The boss will go and talk to the employee, and two things will happen. First, the boss will get to know the employee. Second, the employee will know the Master Corporate Politician shared the credit, and working for the Master Corporate Politician will lead to additional rewards. It will help the Master Corporate Politician when she really wants to do something with that employee because the boss now knows who he is.

Another method I use frequently is to ask for letters of commendation. When something went really well, and I'm basking in the glory of the efforts of my organization, I ask my peer group for selected letters of commendation. By having to write, or at least sign these letters, my peer group recognizes my superstars and will support me when I go to get a promotion or salary increase for them.

Positive visibility for your superstars is important. Always keep their names in front of the bosses with their good deeds. When you need to promote someone, if your superstar is the apparent one, then you won't get some loser friend of the boss; you will get your own person.

Intimidation

> *There are situations in life to which the only satisfactory response is a physically violent one. If you don't make that response, you continually relive the unresolved situation over and over in your life.*
>
> **RUSSELL HOBAN** (b. 1925)

I discuss the antithesis of this in The Screamers and How to Fight Them (see page 37). When all else fails to motivate an employee, you can always revert to the drill-sergeant approach. Screaming and intimidation work. Threats to terminate, discipline, or move to the boneyard are regarded seriously, particularly if you occasionally do it.

Threats that are never carried out soon become useless tools that are ignored. If you must use this tactic to manage an employee, you must be ready to carry out the threat. How many parents use this tactic, but never carry it out by following through? "Johnny, if you don't stop doing that this instant, I'm going to give you a time-out." Does the kid get the time-out if he continues? Most times, no. Does he consider your threat real? Nope! Only when you get up and start walking toward him with the look that says you're really going to do it does he stop the offensive behavior. Employees are the same way. If you threaten and never punish, the threat is useless. You will have to punish to get it done your way.

Intimidation is a very effective tool, but effective only if it is serious and guaranteed to be implemented. The dollar is accepted by all merchants because they know the United States Government stands behind it. If they stood behind it only when they wanted to, then we would have a barter system. Would you work for your corporation if you knew they may or may not honor their implied promise to pay you? Intimidation works the same way. Use it only if you have no other method of managing an employee but, when you do, be prepared to honor it.

If It Were Easy ...

The highest reward that God gives us for good work is the ability to do better work.

ELBERT HUBBARD (1856–1915)

To use this tactic, you need to have a dud in your organization, or one that's readily recognized by all as a dud. A dud is a military term that describes an artillery shell that looks, feels, and acts like a functioning shell, but won't explode. Applied to people, it means they don't function.

I was complaining to my boss one day about how hard my life was. I told him I had so much work to do I didn't think I was ever going to get caught up. I went on and on, and he listened to me silently. When I finished, he looked me in the eye and said, "If it were easy, I would have given the job to Jones." Jones was the dud in our organization. I felt about two inches tall and finished the interview with him as quickly as possible.

What had my boss done to me? He had praised me and he had slapped me down at the same time. He had let me know he knew the job was tough, he had let me know he thought I could do it, and he also let me know he really didn't want to hear any more of my crying about how tough it was. I never complained to him again.

How can you use this on your employees? The guilt it imparts is enough to make them really get moving and quit complaining. I use it now, and it stops the complainers and motivates the superstars. All employees feel they're over-worked and underpaid. They sometimes need reassurance that you know this. The tactic does reassure, and if they're worth a damn, it gets them focused on what you want them to do. Try it!

Esprit de Corps

> *The most important quality in a leader is that of being acknowledged as such.*
>
> **ANDRÉ MAUROIS** (1885–1967)

Why are some organizations a good place to work and others not? Could it be that some organizations have an esprit de corps that makes people want to belong and to be proud to be a part? Why do people continue to join the United States Marine Corps? Is it because they have the most modern equip-ment and the best leadership? No way! People join because to be a marine means something. Being a marine means you're part of the best.

How can a Master Corporate Politician use esprit de corps? He can make people want to be part of his organiza-tion. He can make his people proud they're part of his organ-ization. He can build a feeling that his organization is the best, like the marines, and if you want to be part of the best, join up. It attracts good people because good people want to belong to the good organizations. They don't want to play with a second-rate team—they want to be identified with the best.

How do you do this? You do it by telling everyone you're the best. You convince yourself, your supervisors, and your people that your team is the best. You keep telling them until they believe it themselves and start telling others. Soon, everyone believes it. Are the marines the best? I don't know, but I do know that I, they, and most of the world think they are. They will tell you they are, and if you ask anyone you know which is the most effective fighting force in the world, they will tell you it's the United States Marine Corps. Why? It's because they think they're good, therefore they are good. They demand excellence because it's understood if you're a marine, you're excellent. Excellence is routine, and anything less isn't satisfactory. Use this philosophy with your organization, and you will have one of the best.

Esprit de corps is a heavy responsibility that yields results. It has to be worked on and maintained. You're as good as you think you are. Excellence is expected, and anything less is just not good enough.

Summary

We've covered a lot in this chapter. We've talked about loyalty, ambitious employees, picking the boneyard, and dealing with subordinates. We've looked at tactics that get more from your subordinates, such as expanding something small into something major, and looked at asking subordinates to try a little harder. We've shown that if you want to promote a person, you must keep him or her visible to your management, and we've discussed intimidation to motivate people. I'll never forget when my boss told me, "If it were easy . . ." The final section deals with esprit de corps, and you must have this if your organization is going to succeed.

If you intend to make an organization work for you, then you need to give something back to it. Developing your people and pushing them ahead is the requirement. Don't be afraid to be the boss, and don't be afraid to use your power to help those who are helping you.

chapter 10

Getting Your Share of the Feast

Everyone wants to be promoted, but only a few people a year manage it. Why is that? Is it luck, or did these people do something different? This chapter tells you some of the tricks that Master Corporate Politicians use to ensure they're the one selected for one of the few promotions.

You can just ask for it, or you can become so technically expert that they have to promote you to keep you. You can find another job and force them to promote you, or you can find your boss another job. If you want a promotion, make sure your personnel file is stuffed with letters of commendation from others in the organization. If you're not getting there fast enough, you can always seek employment elsewhere. The best method, the fastest, is to follow a star. When he goes up the org chart, so do you.

Want that promotion? Read on.

Asking for It

If begging should unfortunately be thy lot, knock at the large gates only.

ARAB PROVERB

Don't ask! There are several ways of getting a promotion, and none of them involves directly asking for it. They all require that you make your boss, and perhaps his boss, want to promote you. When you ask a boss for a raise or promotion, one of two things occur in the boss's head. He may think, "Oh, my God, he's right. I need to promote this guy and I haven't done it," or he may think, "Who does this dummy think he is? If he were promotable, I would've already done it." The last thought's the most likely. If the boss wants to promote you, he will find a way. He didn't get to be the boss because he can't get things done, or if he can't, then he knows the big boss real well. If you ask, you will run a great risk of irritating him, and therefore become less promotable in his eyes.

When you ask, the boss is put on the spot. When you put bosses on the spot, they tap-dance, and you don't know what they're thinking. Asking for a raise has to be done with subtlety and finesse. Here's a tactic I used to get a raise:

My Boss: How's it going, Dude?

Me: I'm mad! I just found out I'm in the bottom quartile of my labor grade, and it pisses me off that the company would do that to me. (Notice that I said the company did it to me, not the boss.) It isn't your fault, and I don't expect you to do anything, but I work harder than any of those other guys, and I don't think it's fair.

My Boss: You really think the other guys make more than you do?

Me: You bet your ass, Sir.

My Boss: I will look into it. No promises.

He did look into it, and within a month I received an unscheduled raise. Two things helped: I was on the low end of the scale, and I did work harder. I wasn't confrontational, and I didn't force my boss to do anything. I let him know, when he asked me, what was bothering me. It wasn't his fault, and I led him to believe I didn't think there was anything he could do. He could have answered, "Hey, the pay's handled by personnel. If you got a problem, go see those idiots." Or, he could have answered, "If you want to make more, put out more." There are a lot of tap-dance answers, so be prepared.

Even if the boss can't do anything at the time, he logs it in his memory bank for future reference. He doesn't want to lose you because of pay. The next time he has an opportunity to hand out raises, he will remember that you consider yourself underpaid, and the psychological advantage will be yours.

Timing is very important. If you're subtle when the boss has a lot on his mind or is worrying about a critical issue, the subtlety may go over his head. If you recognize that and make it more overt, and he's not receptive, he'll treat it as if you had come out and directly asked for it. Be careful in your timing. The boss must want to hear you, and you must be subtle. There is nothing I hate more than losing a good employee because of money. Next to that, I hate to hire and train new employees. One thing most people don't realize, particularly those in the lower organizational levels, is that from a boss's perspective, good people are almost impossible to find. New people are hard to train and may not fit into the culture of the organization. The boss doesn't want to lose you if you're a good employee, so you can use this information to your advantage, if you do so with discretion. Be careful, though, because he may not consider you to be one of his good employees.

Become a Technical Expert

A little knowledge that acts is worth infinitely more than much knowledge that is idle.

KAHLIL GIBRAN (1883–1931)

If your boss can find a reason not to promote you, he will, and he will use it. Bosses judge people primarily in four ways when they're considering promotion.

1. Can I get along with this guy? Is he loyal? Do I even like him?

2. Does he understand politics?

3. Can he do the job? Is he a good technician?

4. Can he get along with people? Can he supervise?

Those are a lot of reasons to be rejected. I realized early that I wanted to eliminate as many reasons as I could for rejection. I concentrated on the technical. I obtained a master's degree at night and took the examinations necessary to obtain a professional certification. No one could say I couldn't handle the job technically. I attended many seminars on managing people and adopted the techniques I could that would help me to better manage my people. I'm recognized as a people person. That leaves only two things: Can I get along with my boss? And, do I understand politics?

You, too, can eliminate obstacles to your success. Just reading this book will help you with your political skills. The other aspects of your job can be enhanced by night school and seminars. Getting along with your boss is a personal thing that I can't help you with other than to say that loyalty counts a great deal when it comes to getting along.

Find Another Job

We'll never know the worth of water till the well go dry.

SCOTTISH PROVERB (18TH CENTURY)

As I mentioned earlier, asking for a promotion or a raise has to be done with subtlety, and one of the best ways to say it is by finding another job within the company. I don't recommend you use an outside job offer, as this tells management you're looking to leave. They will probably go ahead and let you, or even make you leave. Finding another job within the company is considered okay because you're a company man and you're just trying to better yourself. When you find another job, the boss has two choices: let you go or promote you so she can keep you.

Just having another department head want you adds to your value. It's kind of like your spouse. If someone tells you what a great body, great mind, great looks, and so on, your spouse has, you appreciate those features and your spouse even more. It works in corporate politics also.

I've seen this technique used successfully many times. I've used it twice, and I've had it used on me by several of my ambitious subordinates. Your boss may tell you she's power-less to promote you, but when faced with losing you to anoth-er department, she can work miracles. By going to her boss and claiming her whole department will collapse, she can get her boss to do something. It works, but you have to be ready to take the other job if it doesn't, or if you've overestimated your worth. Even though you're bluffing, you may have to show your hand.

Find Your Boss Another Job

> *We live in a world of things, and our only connection with them is that we know how to manipulate or to consume them.*
>
> **ERICH FROMM** (1900–80)

A corollary to the previous section is to find your boss a job in either another department or outside the company. When he leaves, that opens up a slot that could be yours, or he may take you with him. Either way, you win.

I had a boss who was just a few years older than I was, and he was the kind of boss that took all of the glory and passed on all of the blame. I wasn't going anywhere under this guy, so I started looking for a job for him. I found out real quick that no one in the company wanted him—his reputa-tion as a jerk was known everywhere except in our organiza-tion—so I had to look outside. I looked for almost three months until I found a job for him that would be a promo-tion, lots more money, and much closer to his home.

I had trouble figuring out how I was going to let him know about it without his knowing I was behind it—it's not good to be known as a manipulator. I used a friend of mine who worked at the company I was trying to place my boss with. He called my boss and told him of the opportunity, and my boss interviewed and got the job. I was promoted to my boss's job and everyone lived happily ever after, except my former boss who was fired six months after he took the job. I guess the new company didn't tolerate jerks as well as we did.

Letters of Commendation

Just praise is only a debt, but flattery is a present.
SAMUEL JOHNSON (1709–84)

I've always found it easier to engineer a promotion for myself or one of my people when I have letters of commendation from other department heads. The letters serve as notice to your boss and perhaps his boss—get them written as high up as you can—that you or the person you're trying to promote is good and he should do something about it. Letters of commendation serve three purposes:

1. They let your management know you did a good job.

2. They let your management know that someone else recognizes your ability and appreciates it.

3. They keep you visible to your management so when promotions become available, your name is on their mind.

To test what I'm telling you, I took an ordinary young man who worked for me and decided to see how fast I could promote him. I obtained letters of commendation from four members of the vice president's staff, and his first promotion went through as if the guy was of divine origin. On another occasion, I wrote a letter for my vice president and talked him into signing it, commending a computer programmer for doing something for me that his management didn't want him to do. The programmer received a promotion rather than a reprimand.

Whenever someone says that I or my organization have done a good job, I ask him to write my boss and my boss's boss—or higher, depending on the level of achievement—a letter saying it. Most people don't mind—those that do, I write the letter for them. It's so rare that the honchos receive a letter, they assume what was done was indeed a masterful piece of work—they really eat it up.

It also helps to recognize the people who help you. Writing letters and copying your boss sends your boss a signal that you are a good manager who gets along well within the organization. If you want to build a team that will follow you, then you need to take care of them. The best way, if you can't give them money, is to see they're recognized by having other people write letters saying what a great job they did.

 # Going Outside for a Job

> It's interesting to leave a place, interesting even to think about it. Leaving reminds us of what we can part with and what we can't, then offers us something new to look forward to, to dream about.
>
> RICHARD FORD (b. 1944)

The first step in getting a job outside is getting an interview. When I run an advertisement in the newspaper, I get fifty to one hundred replies for one job. How do I select whom I will interview and whom I won't? I start weeding them out. The first to go are the guys without college educations. If the stack is still too high, I weed out those who don't have masters degrees. If it's still too high, I look at the resumes themselves to see who's gone to the effort to sell him or herself. I personally don't like professionally prepared resumes because it tells me the person didn't have the ability to do it on his or her own.

When you get the interview, dress as professionally as you can. I've always bought the most expensive three-piece suit I could afford at the time when I determined it was time to change jobs. If my shoes didn't look brand new, then I bought a pair of new ones. The same for a shirt and tie. Get your hair cut at a stylist's two to three days prior to the interview, and if you bite your fingernails, get a manicure and then don't bite them until after the interview. Don't smoke or chew gum.

Answering questions and asking questions is what an interview is all about. You have to relax and realize that, if you're good, the guy interviewing you wants you more than you want him. Don't let him know you know, or he'll think you're an arrogant ass, but let the thought relax you. He's desperate for someone that's good, but he doesn't want to make a mistake and hire a dummy.

You should know as much about the company as you can prior to the interview. Ask questions and take notes, if your interviewer will let you. I always ask if I may, and I've yet to be refused. Taking notes impresses the interviewer because if you write it down, then what he's saying must be important. I always take a list of questions with me when I go in. It shows the interviewer you prepare in advance and aren't one of those impromptu managers. Nothing is as dead as an interview where the guy being interviewed has no questions. It indicates no interest.

They always ask "Why are you looking for a job?" I don't know why they do it, but they do. What they plan on doing with the information is a great mystery. Be prepared to answer it positively. Don't tell him your boss is a jerk or you got screwed at the last salary review or you were passed over for a promotion you thought was rightfully yours or the bastards won't pay you what you're worth. Those type of things tell the interviewer you have an attitude problem, and the last thing he needs is another employee with an attitude problem. A couple of acceptable answers:

- I've always wanted to work for your company, and when I saw your ad, I had to apply.

- I believe there's more opportunity here. I feel I have a lot to offer your company, and I think my experience with my current employer will help me be of great service to you.

Never ask what the job pays. Let them initiate the subject; they will, if they want you. The interviewer will ask you what you make—now's the time to lie through your teeth—and then he may ask, "What's it going to take to get you to come to work for us?" If he does, then what he expects to hear is your price to be 10 to 15 percent above what you're making now. If you ask for more than that, then he will probably reject you because he feels you have an inflated sense of self-worth. Be reasonable in your expectations. If you're not sure you want the job, then add another 10 percent. If he wants you, then he will pay it, but if he's wavering, then you really don't want the job. I took a job once by doing that with a 25 percent increase. I regretted it, but I had named my price, which I thought was too high, and the man accepted it. Don't bluff unless you're willing to pay the price.

Lying is very common on resumes and during interviews. I have a friend who never finished college. You would never know it to talk to him, but his resume says he has a masters. He's never been caught, and he makes more money than I do. When he was a salesman, his resume said he was marketing director. His salary history is always padded by ten thousand dollars a year. Few companies bother to spend the time to verify a person's credentials, and many pay the price for that neglect. Use this knowledge with discretion. I occasionally stretch the truth on resumes and during interviews, but everything I say or write is based on truth and can be verified. I recommend you do the same.

Follow a Star

From time to time there appear on the face of the earth men of rare and consummate excellence, who dazzle us by their virtue, and whose outstanding qualities shed a stupendous light. Like those extraordinary stars of whose origins we are ignorant, and of whose fate, once they have vanished, we know even less, such men have neither forebears nor descendants: they are the whole of their race.

JEAN DE LA BRUYÈRE (1645–96)

Have you ever wondered how Walter Mondale was able to run for the presidency? He was able to because he followed two stars. First, he followed Hubert Humphrey and became a senator and vice president. Then he followed a President, Jimmy Carter, and was allowed to compete for the best job in the world. Did he have talent? Of course, but he followed in the wake of other talented men and rose to a level he may not have achieved had he *not* followed them.

Consider auto racing. Why do the cars get bumper to bumper when they're going one hundred and twenty miles per hour? Do they do it because the drivers are thrill-crazy idiots? No, they do this because they want the front car to break the wind for them, which allows them to follow at the same speed with much less exertion or strain on their engines.

The business world is like politics and auto racing. The easiest way to get to the top is to find a person who is going to the top or is at the top and become one of "his people." If he's rising, the vacuum behind him as he rises will pull you upward with much less effort than if you had to do it all alone. If he's already at the top, it's nice to have a godfather watching out for you.

At certain organizational levels, one's loyalty becomes more important than one's technical ability. In fact, I would rather have a loyal person who's mediocre in ability than a disloyal person who can walk on water. Most top executives think the same way. They take care of the people who are "their people," and they grind into patties the ones that aren't.

Good examples of how following a star can be rewarding occurs almost daily. Large organizations occasionally change leadership for many reasons. When the top person dies, is fired, or leaves for another job, the position, in many cases, is filled from the outside. The person who assumes the top position immediately starts to staff her organization with "her people." It isn't because the people that occupy the vice president and director slots are no good; it's because they're the people of the last boss. The last boss, if he moved to another company, will pull his people along with him and make openings for the new person. If he doesn't pull them along, the new person will gently, or in some cases violently, push them out to make room for "her people."

I've been involved in two incidents of a change in top management. In one case, all but one of the senior executives were fired within a year. In the other, the senior executives were kept on the payroll; they just got new bosses. The new bosses were unable to get along with them, and they voluntarily left. The results were the same: the new boss brought in "his people," and the organization separated into two camps—them and us.

Let's talk about the rewards of following a star from company to company. The money and benefits are always good—it's part of the game. The power is guaranteed because you're one of the boss's people, and you can make immediate changes in screwed-up organizations. Your sense of belonging to a team as contrasted to one person against an organization is good. If the team and the star do well, then you as a member of the star's team will also do well.

What's the downside of this arrangement? If the star goes out, then so do you. Once you start to follow a star, you will have to follow him or her forever or find a new one. It also has an ethical price. Your sense of right and wrong is no longer important. If your star wants it, it must be right. If it's not in the star's best interest, it's wrong. Such conflicts as good for the company versus good for the star are no longer conflicts. The star wins, even if it's bad for the company.

Why do companies have hostile takeovers? Is it because management is altruistic and pure in its desire to protect the stockholder's interests? With tongue in cheek, I say, "Sure!" Takeovers are "hostile" because the guys in power don't want it taken away from them. They aren't representing the stockholders; they're protecting themselves. Does the management ask the stockholders if they want more money for their shares than the market value? Not if they can help it! They fight a takeover for purely selfish reasons.

How about following a star within a single company? This works well until you reach a certain level. At that level, everyone in the star's organization is following the star—senior executives aren't stupid—and then you become just one of the guys and the star will promote based on criteria other than loyalty. I recommend it if you're smart enough to pick a star, but if you guess wrong, then you will spend your career working for a boss who can't get out of middle management.

What do I recommend? I place absolute loyalty with my boss until it conflicts with my own personal interest, or the interest of the company. The interest of the company has to border on fraud or malfeasance before I would turn on my boss. I've turned on two occasions, and I was lucky enough to be right and protected when I did. On both occasions, I left the company because I was no longer considered reliable. They wouldn't fire me, but I couldn't gain a sponsor. No one wanted me on their team.

A friend of mine was talking about a star he was following. The star, the chairman of the board's son, was a bright college kid with the same name as his father. My friend said, "I knew that guy was going somewhere as soon as I heard his name."

Summary

Getting a promotion takes skills and tactics. We've looked at several methods of doing this. We've talked about the merits of asking for it. We've discussed being a technical expert, finding another job, and finding your boss another job. I hope by now you realize the importance of letters of commendation. We discussed going outside for a job, and we discussed following a star. These are a few of the ways to lock down that next promotion opportunity—use them!

chapter **11**

Survival of
the Fittest

Do I like this chapter? Absolutely not! The tactics in this chapter are ones I've seen used, or have had used on me. Read and understand them, then make up your own mind about their use. They are real, and they are nasty.

I will present seven tactics that I consider to be dirty—I don't use them, but they are presented in this book to let you know they exist. These tactics are nonexistent letters, blind copies, letters to the CEO, reprimands and commendations, defective data attacks, calling the government, and let's make a deal. The seven are by no means a comprehensive list. They are all dirty, and if your sense of ethics has already been offended and you don't care if you have a career if it requires knowledge of this, don't read this chapter. However, if you don't read it, be prepared to stay in middle management until you retire, if you can.

Nonexistent Letters

The surest way to be deceived is to consider oneself cleverer than others.

FRANÇOIS, DUC DE LA ROCHEFOUCAULD (1613–80)

I hate this tactic, but I see it used daily. I know the people who use it, and I'm very careful in my dealings with them. Anyone using this tactic is the worst of the Master Corporate Politicians. Generally, Master Corporate Politicians will abide by a code of honor. It may not be one you understand, but they normally have their own code. Anyone using this tactic should be watched very carefully—he or she is dangerous.

What is the tactic? Simple. It's creating letters, after the fact, that cover your ass. If you were too stupid to do it the first time, when it occurred, then do it when you get caught. You create a letter that tells whoever is after you that the problem should be addressed. The real pros will even put the letter into your in box and have it date stamped for you. The date on the stamp? You guessed it; it's at least a month ago.

Does it work? Oh, yeah. It will work because no one believes the disclaimer, "I didn't receive the memo." Would you? The tactic of claiming you didn't receive the letter is so well known that I've not even included it in this book. No one believes it anymore. Don't use it!

How do you combat it? It's difficult if the person sending the letter uses it only occasionally. If it's done frequently, then you may stand a chance of disclaiming it.

Do I recommend it? No, I don't. I know of guys who use this tactic, and I trust them like one would a rabid dog. I hate them, and I do everything I can to destroy them. If a manager doesn't have honor, he has nothing. Honor's a word everyone defines differently, but if you can't be trusted, what good are you? I know a lot of people who will lie to you, but that's within the code. Creating false documents is not. Even liars don't like people who create "after-the-fact" CYA memos.

When should you use it? If the world is coming to an end and you have nothing to lose, or if you need to buy yourself time to escape. The doomsday philosophy may save your life, or it may give you time to find another job.

Do I use this tactic? Never have, and never plan to. I've had it used on me five times, and I've survived without using it. I mention it in this book only to let you know it exists and to alert you to the fact that it may be used on you.

Tactics to combat it? Have your secretary log in all incoming mail. Have her date stamp it and lock up the date stamp when she's not using it. If a letter comes to you, she will know of it, will have logged it, and will have date stamped it. The Master Corporate Politician will have trouble overcoming this defense. If you can afford the effort, direct your secretary to do this. It may keep you out of the grinder.

Blind Copies

The weak in courage is strong in cunning.
WILLIAM BLAKE (1757–1827)

A dirty trick that's been used on me many times is the blind copy. How does it work? It means that the writer of a letter or memo does not advertise the distribution of that document. Normal professional courtesy says you list everyone you're sending a copy of the letter or memorandum to. The Master

Corporate Politician who wants to use this tactic doesn't list them.

What does it do for the Master Corporate Politician? The standard rules of engagement say you work a problem at your level until you can't, and then you go to higher-ups. Using this tactic, you give your opponent the illusion you're following the normal rules, but you aren't. You've inserted his boss, his boss's boss, or even higher into the fight without him even knowing about it. Is it dirty? You bet, but sometimes a Master Corporate Politician may feel it will give him an advantage.

An example of how this tactic was used on me follows:

1. A supplier of mine was shipping product of poor quality— we were shipping it back as fast as he could produce it. He was a small business with a cash-flow problem.

2. The president of the company called me and told me that unless I paid him for his stuff, he was going to write the chairman of the board.

3. I presented our position to him and told him if he had to write a letter to write it to the director of procurement, my boss. He agreed.

4. The bastard did write to my director, but he also sent a blind copy to the chairman of the board and two vice presidents.

5. We paid the man for product we couldn't use just to get the brass off our butts.

Who won? I think he did in the short run, but I did in the long run. I cut that supplier off the bid list, and I've done so in two other companies since then. He may have won the battle, but I will spend the rest of my career ensuring he gets no business from my procurement department. Everyone who's ever worked for me knows about this outfit, and they will never use him. Who won? You tell me.

The only advantage to blind copying a guy is to get a short-term advantage over him. In the long run, he will get even. He may, as I've done, spend a whole career doing it, but he will get even. Should you do it? I don't recommend it, but I've seen it used effectively.

When do you use it? You might use it when all other avenues of reconciliation have failed and you have to have a positive solution to your problem. When it gets down to life or the grinder, you will have to decide.

Letters to the CEO

It's easy to be independent when you've got money. But to be independent when you haven't got a thing— that's the Lord's test.

MAHALIA JACKSON (1911–72)

In the last section I mentioned a supplier who wrote the chairman. Do Master Corporate Politicians like it? Hell, no! You know what it means to have the CEO ask what's happening in your department? It means a great deal of pain for every level of management down to you, and when it gets down to you, the pain is tenfold. Do you want it? Hell, no!

How does it work? It starts by your letter getting to the CEO's office. Chances are she won't see it, but one of her staff assistants will and they will assign it to a group vice president. The group vice president will review it and assign it to a general manager with the notation that the chairman wants an answer. The general manager will assign it to a vice president who will delegate it to a director who will pass it on to a manager. Each pass or delegation adds emphasis to the direction and by the time the CEO's question, "What's this all about?" reaches the cognizant manager, it's been turned into, "Get this damned thing fixed right now!"

Do I recommend a supplier write a letter to the CEO? No, not unless he's written every level up to that position. When he has failed to get satisfaction at each of these levels, then, and only then, should he write the CEO. Every time he moves up a level in the organization, he should send a copy to his buyer and his buyer's supervisor.

What about an employee who's unhappy with the way things work at the subordinate level? If you've got the guts, go for it. You need to be aware that your management will hunt you down and eat you when you do it, but if you have to, do it. There's nothing management hates more than the corporate office looking into a problem with one employee. When they do, the employee is added to the "kill-at-all-cost" list. Every member of management will conspire to snag him, even if it does take a while.

This is a tactic that should be used only once. I've seen a lot of guys use it after they've submitted their termination notice. They tell all the bigwigs and they don't care if there's retribution. Off the record, I encourage my employees to write the letter, particularly if I agree with their views.

Should you do it if you plan on staying on? I recommend you don't because if the Master Corporate Politicians find out who did it, they will toss your bony butt into the grinder so fast you will be amazed. Can you do it without identifying yourself? Maybe, but to have real impact you need to let the CEO know who you are. You can request he keep your name secret, but there's no guarantee. Master Corporate Politicians stick together, even when they're doing wrong. Be careful.

Should you talk to your boss if you're thinking of writing a letter to the CEO? Generally, I'd say no, but there are a lot of honest, hard-working individuals out there who can be trusted. If you work for an honest person—I've only worked for a few in my entire career—then confide in her and let her direct you further.

Will it get action? You bet your sweet buns it will. It may get you burned, but there are a lot of you out there who don't care. If you don't, write the bomb and stand by while it explodes. I often wish I had enough money to tell it like it is. I wish I were stupid enough to write the CEO and tell him how the Master Corporate Politicians he had working for him were wasting his money and how he could make more money if he would only hire workhorses rather than showhorses. Unfortunately, my wife and kids enjoy eating.

Writing the CEO has its risks. If you're secure financially and don't care, or if you're moralistic enough to withstand the aftermath, do it. But if you're like the rest of us, then you can only dream of the independence and the ability to do it.

Reprimand and Commendation

It was beautiful and simple as all truly great swindles are.

O. Henry [William Sydney Porter] (1862–1910)

I would never, in my wildest imagination, have ever conceived this tactic myself. I didn't think it could ever happen to me, but it did. I got slaughtered, and the guy who did it to me is still smiling. I'm patiently waiting for revenge.

What is the tactic? Let me describe it by telling you how I got creamed. I was working on a routine problem when I got a call from a former friend of mine. At the time, we were friends. He told me he had a senior buyer he was going to have to terminate because the man had pissed off the program office. He told me the man was good, but he occasionally had trouble dealing with idiots. My kind of guy, right? He asked me if I would take this guy into my organization since he was a technical expert in procurement and it would be a shame to let a man of his qualifications leave the corporation. I agreed, subject to my former friend's writing me a letter defining the senior buyer's problem and the fact that he had been counseled. I explained I intended to use it only if I had problems with him and, if I didn't, then I would destroy the letter. My former friend agreed and wrote the letter. In less than two weeks, I knew I had a dud, and I had to get rid of him. Guess what? The son of a bitch that used to be my friend wrote a letter of commendation for the senior buyer making it impossible for me to fire him. I was stuck with a dud, and I couldn't use the letter I had planned to use to grind him into patties because in the employee's personnel file was this glowing letter of commendation.

What did I do? I found him a job with another company making almost 25 percent more than I was paying him. I still hate the former friend who did this to me, but I'm beginning to mellow a little. If I had a loser as an employee, what would I do to get rid of him? Would I have done the same thing? Maybe, but I would never have written the commendation letter.

If you want to destroy a guy, unload your losers on him, then write them letters of commendation. He can't fire them when they have such glowing letters in their personnel files. He can't do anything other than find them another job. If you want to make an enemy for life or get even, use this tactic.

Defective Data Attack

McCarthyism is Americanism with its sleeves rolled.
JOSEPH MCCARTHY (1908–57)

How is it that Senator Joe McCarthy was able to buffalo the entire nation when he didn't have a single shred of evidence? Why is it that people accept assertions without verifying their validity? I can't explain it, but people are that way. They're willing to accept the most foul accusation if it suits their purpose. Even if they have no motive of their own, they will believe the worst in a person. Think about it a minute. If you're a man, and another man tells you a certain female is easy, do you believe it? Probably. Why? I don't know, but I would. I guess it's because I want to. Sometimes we just want to think the worst of someone, even someone we like.

If you've gotten this far in the book, you have a good idea of what corporate politics is all about. What did the last paragraph say? I'll tell you—it revealed a gold mine. It told you how to get rich and not have to work at it, *if* you have no ethics.

Want to ruin a person? Start rumors—any sort of rumor. People will want to believe it. If enough do, it becomes true, even if it is totally untrue. You can't escape the opinions of the masses, regardless of how erroneous they are. You've heard this one before: Perception is reality. Some rumors people use to destroy a man are:

- He beats his wife.

- He fools around with anything that will let him.

- He's been married four times before.

- He was in a mental institution.

- He likes kinky sex—whips, chains, etc.

How do they ruin a woman? They label her as easy. They tell everyone she puts out on the first date and that she will do anything to get ahead. Guess what? Everyone will believe it, and she will have trouble getting ahead. If she does get ahead, everyone will say she got there because she did something that's not talked about. She can't win. Other rumors they might use:

- She has an illegitimate child.

- She had an abortion.

- She does drugs.

- She sells her body.

If someone wanted to ruin an organization, how would he go about it? He would try by attacking the senior personnel. If the senior personnel are untouchable, then he would start working his way down. The examples listed here aren't the only ones he could use to defame a person. If he were to put his mind to it, I'm sure he could come up with some whoppers that would destroy even the most principled person. The most vulnerable are often those who appear to be the most untouchable. When you have a man who doesn't fool around on his wife, he's a homosexual. A woman who doesn't date people in the office is a lesbian. Given enough time, these bastards' twisted minds will come up with something capable of destroying even the most solid citizen.

This tactic isn't limited to personal attacks. It is used to make assaults of a professional nature. If these people need some data that's not available, they create it. If they are being harassed by someone they want to go away, they can blunt the attack by creating data that proves this person doesn't know what she's doing.

Women have a tactic that men don't. Men are hard-pressed to file a sexual harassment suit, but women can. Go ahead—watch them laugh. If a man is charged with rape, he can deny it, but who will believe him? Women have a weapon that men have serious trouble defending themselves against. If they want revenge, they can get it. If a woman accuses, then the man's generally guilty, period. Innocent or not—guilty, end of story. If he didn't do it, he *wanted* to do it. If a woman wants to make sure a man gets ground up, she can have a girl-friend say that he harassed her, too. Be careful, it happens—and it works. Even the threat of it works.

Do I use these tactics? No. I don't have to, I don't want to, and even the thought of it sours my stomach. But, if I got cornered like a rat and knew I was going to get executed, then I might consider it. As a Master Corporate Politician, survival is the foremost thing on my mind, but I do have to look at myself in the mirror in the morning

Don't use this tactic unless you have to, but be aware of it. And if you're a man pray your female employees don't read this chapter.

Call the Government

I don't know jokes; I just watch the government and report the facts.

WILL ROGERS (1879–1935)

There must be a million different local, state, and federal agencies assigned to protect us from the bad boys in corporations. Think about it. We've got OSHA, EPA, LRB, EEOC, NRC, DCAS, DCAA, Health and Sanitation, Wage and Hour, building inspectors, and on and on. The government's decided it's going to get involved in your life and help you.

As a Master Corporate Politician, what does this mean to you? It means one more entity to carry out a Master Corporate Politician's dirty work. I don't recommend it because once you use it, you will never work anywhere again. I've included this tactic in this chapter because there are people who use it, and you need to be aware.

Got a boss who needs a few problems so he will get off your back? Make an anonymous phone call to the appropriate government agency. The government guys will work him over good. Want to punish the general manager? Look around your facility and note the violations. There are violations, millions of them, because there are too many laws to adhere to all of them. When you get a few violations and can document them, call the government. If you don't need to document them, for something like asbestos falling off the wall, just call the government and tell them where to find it.

A friend of mine quit a company, disgusted with the management, because they wouldn't follow all the laws and were typical greedy corporate scrooges—his management claimed they couldn't afford to follow all the laws. He was so angry that before he left, he made notes of all the violations he was aware of. The day he quit, he phoned every agency in the phone book. His former company has paid more in fines, lost work, and inconvenience than if they had just spent the money to bring themselves into compliance with the law in the first place.

This tactic is nasty, but if you want to punish or seek revenge, this is the one for you. The government guys will usually allow you to remain anonymous and will do your dirty work for you; but if word gets out that you did this, prepare to kiss a paycheck goodbye.

Let's Make a Deal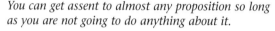

You can get assent to almost any proposition so long as you are not going to do anything about it.
JOHN JAY CHAPMAN (1862–1933)

Another former friend of mine did this to me, and I still hate his guts for it. I look forward to the time when I can return the favor. The only reason I remained with that employer so long was the opportunity to get revenge. I left before I got it. I knew that if I stayed long enough, that my former friend would have to work for me again. I was like a spider—waiting for my opportunity to strike back.

What did he do to make me so mad? He double-crossed me. We had a deal, he let me perform my end of it, and then he arranged it so he didn't have to do his. Nice guy, right?

Here's what happened. I needed a subcontract administrator, and he needed a sheet-metal buyer. I had what he needed, and he had what I needed. The people involved both wanted to change because there was more money in it for both of them. I transferred my guy, and my former friend didn't promote his person. She no longer wanted to come. I got screwed. Did my former friend do it intentionally? I'm sure. Did he get what he wanted, which was to take my person and not give up one of his? Yes. I got beaten by a Master Corporate Politician.

The point of the section on tactics is that if you don't mind a little risk, you can double-cross people and get what you want. Make a deal, then do whatever you want. This is a good tactic to use one time, when you have to win. After using it, no one will ever trust you again, and they may be like me—waiting to chop off your head. There are no police departments in corporate politics, and no courts of appeal.

Summary

A Master Corporate Politician will lie, steal, and double-cross to get his or her way. If you don't believe it, reread this chapter. Dirty tricks are the things a Master Corporate Politician uses to get even, to punish, or to just win. They will create nonexistent letters, send blind copies, write letters to the CEO, reprimand and then commend, use defective data, call the government, and make a deal. Would you buy a used car from one of these guys?

chapter 12

Learn to Spot Traps and Use Them to Your Advantage

This chapter deals with the ways a Master Corporate Politician can use the organization (org) chart to ruin a subordinate's career or enhance it if he is one of the favored few. It is one of the most common ways in which the Master Corporate Politician destroys those subordinates who are not loyal. He can also destroy loyal people inadvertently because he is not aware of the ramifications of some of these organizational dynamics. An org chart, detailing who works where, and for whom, is a powerful weapon that either helps the subordinate accomplish the organizational goals (the Master Corporate Politician's goals), or impede them. The astute

Master Corporate Politician will organize her staff to accomplish what she wants accomplished. If it is to ruin a disloyal subordinate, then the organization will be set up that way. If she wants to actually accomplish something, then it will be set up another way. Or, if the Master Corporate Politician intends to help promote a favorite subordinate, then you can guess how the organization will be set up—all the horsepower will reside with the favored son.

I once worked for a company that changed org charts every month. When I asked why, it was always the "We need some new ideas around here," or "We need to fix this problem, and the guy running it isn't cutting the mustard." As I explained earlier, a changing org chart is like a moving target for the Master Corporate Politician. If the people keep changing, then it gives the appearance to onlookers that management is trying to fix the problem. "We just didn't have the right guy in the slot—we have the right guy now. Things are going to smooth out—trust us!" If the guy to blame for the problem is turned to meat and replaced by another, then the observer believes that justice has been done, and that "tomorrow is another day."

Organizations work only when the Master Corporate Politician wants them to work. If he wants them to succeed, then you can rest assured that unless he is incompetent, they will work. A Master Corporate Politician will do whatever it takes to get his wishes, and if his wishes are for a functional organization, then the organization will function. If he is trying to grind up a subordinate or two, then the organization will be dysfunctional until they are beef patties.

If you can master the tactics in this chapter, then you are well on your way to being a Master Corporate Politician. Read on to learn how to organize a subordinate out of a job, into a nothing job, or to humiliate. Learn how to create organizations and systems that are doomed to fail, organizations that slowly take away a subordinate's staff, and that burn out a subordinate. This chapter also discusses how to starve a subordinate to death, staff her with idiots or with people who are not loyal to her. If you are trying to survive, then you better fully understand what these tactics are and be prepared to handle them when they are thrown in your direction. Because, whatever your objectives, THEY ARE COMING YOUR WAY!

Organize the Subordinate Out of a Job

> *Under all conditions well-organized violence seems to him the shortest distance between two points.*
>
> LEON TROTSKY (1879–40)

Everyone needs to feel he or she has some value. No work, no assignments, nothing to do makes a person feel useless. Since he or she is doing nothing for you, he or she is useless. What do you do with useless people? You get rid of them—you grind them into patties.

Do you ever have lulls in your work where you don't have anything to do? Or, are there times when all that you have to do is a bunch of small odds and ends that can wait forever? If you are like me, then it is at this point that I get very uneasy. I like it when the work is hard and the pace is frantic. When things slow down, then I become uncomfortable with myself. It's almost as if I am not contributing as much as I should. I watch the other guys scrambling around and I want to be part of the action. I want to be a player.

There have been times when I sat for months with nothing to do. I was caught in a management shake-up and put out to pasture. Put out to pasture means they let you stay employed until you can find a job—you may get a few special assignments, but no permanent work. I sat in my office and stared at the ceiling. It was a horrible feeling. I was drawing a paycheck and doing nothing for it. Management wasn't about to fire me, but they weren't going to give me any meaningful work. Did they want me to quit? Absolutely, but I had been assured that they weren't going to fire me. I was safe until the bean counters decided that we needed another head-count reduction to get the overhead back in line. I knew my name was going to be on the top of that list. I updated my resume and took the first job offering me more money. Their tactic worked on me.

The way it works is that a Master Corporate Politician takes away a guy's responsibilities so that the subordinate has nothing to do and lets everyone know he doesn't. When staff-reduction time rolls around, and it does every year as the general manager assesses his performance to budget, then the subordinate is vulnerable. The Master Corporate Politician won't have any trouble convincing his boss that this is the guy to toss over the transom. It may happen long before that if the Master Corporate Politician has really destroyed the guy's image or if the Master Corporate Politician has managed it such that the subordinate really pissed off the management. They may just give him ninety days to find a job, or else. Either way, the Master Corporate Politician has won, and the guy is gone.

My first experience of this tactic occurred two years into my career. I was a young college grad working hard to make it into management. The man I am using as an example had been the department manager a few months ago. He had been whipped, and it showed in his face. My friends and I (before management, I did have friends) watched this guy for months—he didn't do anything. Nothing! One of the women working with us told us what he made (his salary), and we were amazed. This man made more money than God and almost as much as Bill Gates, and he did nothing. He came in on time, and left on time but did nothing. He just sat there!

How can this be? you ask. Don't corporations require that their employees perform? Yes, they do, but they don't require anything from a guy put out to pasture. These guys are allowed to just graze on the grass and slowly die. The longer they stay around, the leaner the grass becomes, and ultimately, disappears—as do they.

When it happened to me, I left before the ax fell. But I have seen other guys who were put out to pasture who stayed there and slowly worked their way back into favor. It's a long, hard road, but it can be done. How did they do it? Since they have a great deal of free time on their hands, they can concentrate on a problem and really wear it out. They can fix things that the line and staff guys don't have time to mess with. They can take on systems-implementation projects that nobody else wants and do a first-class job on them. They can fix things that no one else can because of their unique skills. The solution to being put out to pasture is to find productive work in the environment that expelled you and then excel.

Another good example of this happened with an older gentleman who was the production control (PC) manager of a manufacturing plant. The new management came in and they didn't want him—he was too much of the old culture. They couldn't fire him because he had twenty-plus years with the company, so they slid him out to pasture. In his long career, this guy had worked himself up from an factory expediter to PC manager and he knew the plant as if he had designed it. He knew how everything worked, and just about everybody owed him something. The new management didn't owe him a thing except an office in the back of the building.

We were having trouble with part shortages. The fancy computer system we had installed wasn't working up to spec, and we were awash in shortages. I tried to duck the problem, but my boss assigned me to the tiger team to clean up the shortage problem and do it fast. He had made it clear that our careers depended on it. As he put it, "This is a bet-your-career assignment." In other words, you either perform, or your residence will be changed to the local meat market as a product therein. I wasn't the lead guy on the team, just a member, and we applied massive amounts of manpower to the task. One of the first things you learn in business is that manpower, if applied in sufficient quantity, will solve any problem. Sometimes it's like saying if it takes a woman nine months to create a child, then if you get nine women, you can have a child in one month. Well, this problem was just like the last example. Nine women can't make a baby in one month, and the hordes of expediters we put on the shortage problem couldn't solve it either.

How did we finally solve the problem? We brought the old PC guy into the tiger team and listened to him. He had been building the product for years and knew all the angles. Three months after we had him on board, the shortages were reduced to what management could accept.

How do you survive when they've put you out to pasture? You call in all the markers from everyone you know and hope you can get another productive assignment. If, or when, you get that opportunity, you better do damned well. If you can't get another job, or can't do extremely well at the one you did get, then they've won, and you better find another job pretty quick, or you will hear your flesh as it sizzles on the grill.

Organize the Subordinate into a Nothing Job

> *The gods had condemned Sisyphus to ceaselessly rolling a rock to the top of a mountain, whence the stone would fall back of its own weight. They had thought with some reason that there is no more dreadful punishment than futile and hopeless labor.*
>
> **ALBERT CAMUS** (1913–60)

When I got creamed a few years ago, the Master Corporate Politician who had brought me to my knees didn't have enough on me to fire me, so he demoted me. He really demoted me. I was the materials manager, and he put me down to being a financial analyst. Quite a fall. From the lofty heights of executive row to the dirty trenches of bean-count world. I was put there to be humiliated and embarrassed and was allowed to find another job.

I didn't quit—I stayed on, and on, and on. I stayed in the position for almost six years. Did they accomplish their objectives? No, I wouldn't leave. Did I accomplish my objectives? Yes, I was trying to put four kids through high school without having to disrupt their lives by moving them to another city.

Other guys don't look at it this way. They let their pride get in the way of common sense. They get demoted, and they bail out as soon as something comes along. A boss of mine got creamed, and he pulled out immediately to a job demanding far less than what he was capable of—he hated it and then moved again in about a year. Most people need to have peer recognition. When a Master Corporate Politician puts you into the barrel, then you have to ask yourself if this is important to you. It will hurt your pride and you will suffer. But, can you live with it until you decide where you want to go next? Stay put and assess the situation with cool detachment. The Master Corporate Politician got you, and you are now one of the subordinates. You can either work your way back up, stay put and enjoy life for a while, or you can jump ship and go elsewhere. I stayed, and I'm working my way back up. Three of my children graduated from the same high school, and the fourth is starting there. I got out of the barrel two years ago, and my career is starting to resemble the one I had before I got creamed.

Remember one thing, a very important thing: Management changes all the time. In a few years the guys who took a knife to your career either have been eaten by bigger fish and are working in the next cubicle over or have moved on. The new management doesn't remember your sins, and they are always looking for guys who can fit into their team and get the job done.

Another friend of mine got dished the same poison I did, and she did the same thing I did. She stayed. She was the controller, and she got demoted. Did she jump ship? No, she stayed put. She is getting her kids through high school and college and collecting retirement points. I expect that together, in about five years, we can flip them the finger and then go do something else. Consider it, particularly if you are over forty.

Why don't they just fire you? Why keep you on the payroll? Why not just cut off your head, hand it to you, and then march your butt out the door? Why would they be so kind as to give you a menial position? The answer is the personnel (human resources, as they like to call themselves) department. The people in personnel won't let them fire you unless they have an ironclad case of incompetence, and the definition of ironclad changes every time you go to see them. Remember, they're idiots. So, from the Master Corporate Politician's perspective, it is easier to put you out to pasture to either die or find another job than it is to figure out what is an ironclad case.

I watched one of the finest men I have ever known get organized out of his job, his life, and his manhood. He was a maverick, no college, but one of the smartest men I have ever worked for. He knew how to manage people, and he knew how to get the job done. A real pro, and a pleasure to work for. The bastards got him.

Single-handedly, in my opinion, this man had saved our plant from being shut down. He set standards for the engineering department and imposed schedules on them (the first and only time I have seen this), developed computerized bills of material to order from, organized the procurement department to ensure that the parts were ordered on time, and restructured receiving and inspection to where they weren't the traditional black holes. In a few words, he had fixed our problems and set us on the road to recovery. We were almost there when new management arrived.

New management means new people. One truth you can take from this book is the first sentence in this paragraph. My hero was old people, and he "just didn't fit in" to the new culture. They got him and organized him into the back forty—nowhere land.

True to the promise to the old owners, they didn't fire him, but they stole his self-respect, his ability to do anything, and his life. He killed himself a few years later, and I think it was as a direct result of the treatment given him by the new management; it had scarred him permanently. He was taken out to pasture and allowed to eat the grass and die. Die he did.

I liked this guy more than any other boss I have ever had. He was ethical, and his objectives were always honorable—the only Master Corporate Politician I have ever met who was not a traditional Master Corporate Politician. I have spent the time since his death trying to live up to his standards. I only wish I had his strength of character and ability.

When I was in Vietnam, I was in my early twenties. I didn't think I could be killed. I guess I was right, because I'm still here. As a young executive, I'm sure you feel the same way: invulnerable. I'm sure you are cocky, self-confident, and almost arrogant in your assessment of your ability. Guess what? I was the same way. In my first ten years, I quadrupled my salary—I was *the* definition of fast track and I was on my way to a vice presidency. I was smart, educated, and I knew how to get things done. They referred to me as "the wizard," or as they do now, as "the professor." I know how to do everything. Jack of all trades, master of most—if not all. I got beaten and stuck into a nothing job, and you will too if you let your ego get in the way of remembering the corporate rules. I forgot Rule #1 (see page 2). Forget it, and you will find yourself in the barrel, and then you will have to decide what is important to you. A life, or a career? The cook, or the meat?

 # Create an Organization Doomed to Fail

> *There is not a fiercer hell than the failure in a great object.*
>
> JOHN KEATS (1795–1821)

One of the Master Corporate Politician's most potent weapons is the organization (org) chart. With this piece of paper, she can make or break your career. She can assign all the aces to you and all the idiots to the other guys, or anything she wants. With an org chart, a Master Corporate Politician controls your career. If you are in charge of bringing in a complex computer system, she can assign the programmers to you, or she can give them to someone else and have them matrixed to you. The difference? The difference is that if they don't work for you, they work for somebody else, and that somebody is the one who calls the tune on their priorities.

Master Corporate Politicians use this weapon with the precision of a surgeon. If they have a guy they want gone, and they always do or I wouldn't be able to write this book, then they adjust the org chart to where the subordinate of choice cannot be effective. Here's a classic example. I took over a materials manager's job from a guy who had been having a running gun battle with a Master Corporate Politician. The Master Corporate Politician finally won; I was hired, and the other guy moved out to pasture. The organization was designed to fail. All the buyers and their supervisors worked for the functional guy. They reported to me on a programmatic basis, but the solid line was with the functional guy. The functional guy's priorities were with another program, not mine. The organization had been set up to destroy my predecessor, and it did. When I complained about it, the boss gave me direct reporting.

Here's another example of how an org chart can kill you. When the shortage situation got so bad that something had to be done, there were two choices for management. They could reorganize so that procurement took control of the shortages since most were all procurement related, or they could give the task to production control (PC). The plant manager at the time hated the director of procurement, so guess who got the task? PC started to immediately blame all late shipments on procurement. It wasn't long before the procurement director was in hot water with the big dogs. She wasn't able to fix the problem because he didn't control the organization that reported the status. Whatever she did, however good she was, the reports were always negative. She got replaced.

Another example. The guy who replaced the director of procurement in the previous example was liked by the plant manager. When the new director suggested that PC and procurement be merged into one department, it was accepted. After that, the shortage problem went away. The new director controlled the information and status, and it was now always an engineering problem. The engineering arrived late, it was no good, nobody could make it, the lead times on source control drawings were a lifetime plus some, and so on. Engineering was now the bad guys.

An example of setting up an organization to fail occurred when I was assigned to implement a new computer system to define and schedule our material requirements. I was given the fancy title of program manager, but no one reported to me. This is a position, program manager, that I refer to many times in this book. Depending on the organization, it can be many things. Generally, they are the guys who own a particular program or task and are responsible for "making it happen." They generally own the budget, can authorize people to do work, and are held accountable to meet schedule. Other terms for this position are business manager, unit manager, product-line manager. In this new position, everybody reported to me on a dotted line, but there was no solid-line reporting. My job was to get the system, define the changes needed to make it work in our environment, ensure the changes happened, train the users, and then implement the system. No problem, right? Nobody wanted the system except my boss's boss. I was swimming upstream, and I wasn't going anywhere. When I complained to my boss, he just laughed at me. I had been organized to fail, and I failed.

Another example of how a Master Corporate Politician will screw you over when he puts an org chart together occurred in the movie, *Twelve O'clock High*. In this movie, Gregory Peck, a general, assigns all the losers to one unit. Even the officer in charge of that unit is considered a loser. What the general wanted to do was shame the losers into greater output and better performance. What a Master Corporate Politician wants is for all of them to fail. I saw this happen in corporate life. My director set up a group called the Special Projects Team. On that team, he put every loser he had and anyone he didn't like. Their assignment was to implement the new computer system. Guess what? The boss didn't give them any direction on what he wanted, so they didn't do anything. The boss rented a trailer so he could get them out of the main factory, and in time, nobody knew them anymore. He was able to lay them off, one by one. How did he do this? He used an org chart to grind up the people he wanted gone.

Another way Master Corporate Politicians use an org chart for assassination is by assigning a guy a task and not giving him the horsepower to get the job done. I already mentioned an example, but this is the most common way a Master Corporate Politician gets rid of a subordinate. Have an engineering problem, assign a guy to go fix it. Don't give him the engineering liaison people, just let him go out there and fix it. When he fails, then you can either write him up or fire him. If Master Corporate Politician has a problem with vendor shortages, he doesn't tell procurement that they have to cooperate with his guy—just let him figure out how to fix it without their help. When he fails, and he will because procurement is very territorial and will resist all his efforts, the Master Corporate Politician will gleefully flip the switch on the grinder.

If a Master Corporate Politician wants one of his guys to succeed, then the org chart is modified to where that subordinate gets all the horsepower he needs. Not only does this guy get the support of the Master Corporate Politician, he gets the org chart changed to where he really doesn't need it. We call it a magic-carpet ride—a ride to promotion. If a Master Corporate Politician doesn't want a guy to succeed, then the org chart is fixed so that anybody he needs works for someone else. We call this the kamikaze ride—a one-way trip to hell. The Master Corporate Politician will arrange the org chart to ensure that whatever she wants to happen, will happen.

What do you do if the org chart is an upwind sail? You can ask for it to be fixed, and if it was just an oversight on your boss's part, he may fix it for you. If he has set it up that way intentionally, then you are wasting your time, and his. You can go whine to the idiots in personnel, but all they can (or will) do is wring their hankies with you. You can note it in your diary that you tried both your boss and personnel, but when you fail, you have failed. What do you do when the boss has decided to stack the org chart against you? You kiss your butt good-bye because you are dead.

Away a Little at a Time

> When sorrows come they come not single spies,
> But in battalions.
>
> **WILLIAM SHAKESPEARE** (1564–1616)

It's like peeling an artichoke, one leaf at a time. That is how a Master Corporate Politician will disassemble a subordinate's organization. If he does it in one stroke, then he might be accused of being unfair or unkind to the subordinate. If he peels it away a leaf at a time, then with each leaf he has a plausible excuse or a good organizational reason.

A few years ago, my boss did this to me. He was after me, and I was too well wired up the chain of command for him to just move me out to pasture. He had to take me down a little at a time. His first move was to take away the subcontract of our biggest supplier. His rationale was that it was so big, it needed extra supervision and control. He hired a senior engineer and put him on his staff and assigned the subcontract administrator, a guy who used to work for me, to this engineer. I fought it, but my functional boss didn't care, and I lost. With this move, the Master Corporate Politician had taken away half the procurement dollars I was spending and placed it under another's control.

The next thing he did was to take shipping and receiving and place them under the control of manufacturing. The rationale here was that my job was to get the parts to the back door, and after that it was the job of manufacturing to move them wherever they wanted them. I fought it, and like the last battle, I lost. With this move, he had taken away half the staff I had working for me.

His next move was going to be to take the material-planning function and give it to production control. I didn't survive in that position long enough for him to do it, but that was his next move. I also learned he was planning to hire more engineers on his staff and was planning to assign my buyers to them, leaving me only the administration function, which he could eliminate at a later time. It was only a matter of time until this guy had plucked me like an artichoke. Were these motives to get rid of me? Or legitimate business decisions? Who knows? I viewed it as the former.

EAT—OR BE EATEN

Does it work? It sure was working on me. I was defense-less to stop him. If I had worked for a different functional boss, then I don't think it would ever have happened, but anything is possible in the world of corporate politics. If one Master Corporate Politician makes a strong enough case that something needs to be changed, then the other Master Corporate Politicians will generally get out of his way.

I must admit that I have used this tactic myself on my subordinates. When I have people who are not performing, then I can't continue to let them not perform—my survival depends on performance. When they are not meeting spec, then I tend to take things away from them until they can per-form to specifications with what they have. If they can't meet spec on anything, then ultimately, nothing is all they will have to do. When they are doing nothing for me, then I don't need them, and I start looking for ways to get rid of them. The sword cuts both ways.

To fight it? I had another experience where my boss was trying to destroy me by taking away my organization, a matrix position with ten direct reports. This time, I joined forces with him and off-loaded the entire organization back to his func-tional managers. He thought he had me, but it went the other way. Since I no longer had any people, I wasn't responsible for anything—his people were accountable to me to get things done, and when they didn't, I dropped grenades in his office. I began to just wear him out with his organization's inability to support me and the program I was assigned to. The tactic backfired on him, the program people came to my defense, and we beat him up so badly that the entire organization that supported me was reassigned back to me and taken complete-ly out of his control. Again, the sword cuts both ways.

Another example (different company) occurred when my director, the director of procurement, fell from favor with the vice president of material. The director had transferred out of the corporate office, which presented a challenge for the vice president—you can't just kill people wired into heaven. The approach the VP took was to slowly take chunks of the directorate and give them to the other directors.

Since material shortages are always a problem, this is a logical first step. The VP took all the follow-up people and assigned them to the material-operations director. The rationale was that since the material-operations people were closer to the problem, the factory, they would have more enthusiasm and pursue the vendors much more aggressively. Also, this would allow the procurement director to focus more on meeting the aggressive material cost budget. This took about a quarter of the director of procurement's staff away.

The next area the VP looked at was the engineering liaison group. This group was chartered with working out the engineering problems encountered by the procurement group, working engineering changes with the suppliers, putting bid packages together, and establishing configuration control on purchased parts. They accounted for about 10 percent of the staff of procurement. The logic to moving these guys was that the director of material planning had come out of engineering. What better sense than to put these guys to work for a person who knew the engineering organization inside and out. The VP did this, and now my director was down to half his previous size.

The next move was the material-estimating group. These people prepared proposals and estimates and tracked performance to them. The VP created a new directorate to accomplish this, the material-estimating and control group. Zap, another 10 percent of the procurement director's staff went to another.

The next move? The VP split up the procurement organization into two directorates, one for major subcontracts and the other for the ash and trash (off the shelf and commodities). The major subcontracts group handled 90 percent of the dollars and 10 percent of the parts—they were the glamour group. Guess who got the ash and trash group? You got it, the original director of procurement. When the original director was reduced to having only the commodity buyers, or about 15 percent of his original staff, the VP had him surrounded, and it was only a matter of time before he folded his tent and left the organization.

This tactic works and works surprisingly well. When a Master Corporate Politician wants to cut a subordinate out of his organization, he can do it one leaf at a time. Like a tree, he can cut it down with an ax, or he can pluck off all its leaves one at a time and watch it slowly die. Either way, the subordinate is going to die.

Burn the Subordinate Out

In order that people may be happy in their work, these three things are needed; They must be fit for it; they must not do too much of it: and they must have a sense of success in it—not a doubtful sense, such as needs some testimony of others for its confirmation, but a sure sense, or rather knowledge, that so much work has been done well, and fruitfully done, whatever the world may say or think about it.

W. H. AUDEN (1907–73)

Burn him out is where the Master Corporate Politician loads up the subordinate to the point where she can't get it all done. He just keeps giving the subordinate larger and larger portions of the organization, or more and more assignments. The more organization or tasks she has, the more areas where the Master Corporate Politician can find fault. This is particularly useful to the Master Corporate Politician when he has a subordinate who is truly competent and capable of doing the job. If she's capable in one area, then the Master Corporate Politician will give her other areas where she may not be so capable. In effect, the Master Corporate Politician keeps giving her organizational pieces until he finds an area where he can attack the subordinate.

There are generally two results of this type of tactic. First, the Master Corporate Politician finds something where the subordinate does not excel and then starts the standard campaign to get rid of her. Or, the subordinate does excel, and then the Master Corporate Politician is at risk himself because the subordinate has proven she can do anything assigned to her. If she has most of the boss's organization working for her, then what do the big dogs need with the boss? Risky? Yes.

I saw this used early in my career, and I don't know if it was the intent of the Master Corporate Politician to load the person up and burn him out, or if he was just desperate to get a subordinate who could get things done. My boss was in charge of material operations, primarily a warehousing function. He took over production control, and then purchasing. He owned most of his boss's organization when it was over. He ultimately became the vice president, so if this was a tactic by his boss, it didn't work. My boss then was a very astute Master Corporate Politician, and I think he is one of the inspirations for this book—many of his tactics are showcased here. Just watching him move was awe inspiring.

Here's another example: My boss then, the director of materials, had a guy running the warehouse operation. We called him Flash because he was dull in speech and action, mediocre, but competent. When I started complaining about the "black hole" in receiving and receiving inspection (not then working for Flash), my boss (and his too) assigned receiving inspection to Flash. We called it the black hole because parts would go in and never come out. Things didn't get any better with Flash running things; they got worse. I was all over this guy and was demanding that something be done to fix the black hole. Daily, I creamed Flash with items critical to production that had been sitting in his new area for weeks. Based on my complaint, our boss moved Flash into oblivion with a nothing job on the other side of the factory. The next guy knew what he was doing, and the problem went away. My boss got what he wanted, which was a new man to run the warehouse and receiving area, and I got what I wanted, which was timely movement of parts. Everybody won except Flash, the poor mediocre warehouse guy.

Another variant of this tactic is what I call "musical chairs." Musical chairs is where the Master Corporate Politician rotates the management around. Manager A and Manager B switch jobs. Sounds like a good idea, doesn't it? Each manager benefits from learning the other's job. It makes for a stronger organization, improves each subordinate's background, and makes for a more qualified staff. You can guess the real reason a Master Corporate Politician would use this, can't you? Yes, sir! The real reason a Master Corporate Politician does this is to move one of his subordinates into a job she cannot perform.

I have seen musical chairs done numerous times. One of the first times was when my manager (he ran the warehouses) and a man named Bob, the manager of planning (a direct report to the VP also), were having turf wars. Since procurement was screwed up at the time (and it always is in someone's perspective), my manager convinced the VP to move Bob (we called him Sweet Old Bob, a.k.a. SOB) into procurement working for the procurement director. Bob's replacement was, you guessed it, one of my manager's boys. The rationale used to move SOB, and it really couldn't be argued with, was that procurement needed the horsepower that SOB would bring to the procurement organization. SOB, although a senior executive with many year's experience, had never worked in Procurement and knew nothing about it. Bob flopped around like a fresh-caught fish on the bottom of a boat. He tried, but he had no background in the problems he was facing, and it wasn't long before he was meat.

To make things even worse (or better, depending on your perspective) for SOB, my manager also convinced the VP that it would be a good idea to give Bob some experienced help—me. This was an easy sell to the VP because I was recognized at that time as a hot-shot dude who could do anything. But I, too, had never worked in procurement. With half of SOB's staff working for me, and the other half working for a guy of marginal ability, it added an extra layer of dry rub to Sweet Old Bob's grilling. My manager never discussed it with me, but I suspect his plans were for me to succeed Bob when the grilling was over. When SOB was safely eating his grass in pastureland, I would have half the procurement organization working for me while being loyal to him. I left the company before this happened, but my replacement ultimately became the director of procurement working for my former manager who had ascended to the vice presidency.

Good things do happen to good people. My former manager moved on to bigger and better things after making vice president. Sweet Old Bob came back in favor with the new management—he got out of pastureland—and ultimately became a vice president. A good end for a good man.

How do you defend against it? You do as my boss did in the first example—you succeed. If you don't, then plan on living your life in a pasture somewhere with nothing to do. Live there until they need some head-count reductions and then plan on your head being one of the reductions. You can't refuse to accept additional organizational responsibilities because if you do, then the offers of more will stop. You will find yourself, as Peter Drucker puts it, "Terminally placed." That means you don't go anywhere—*ever!*

Organize to Humiliate/Reward/Punish

> One of the many reasons for the bewildering and tragic character of human existence is the fact that social organization is at once necessary and fatal. Men are forever creating such organizations for their own convenience and forever finding themselves the victims of their home-made monsters.
>
> ALDOUS HUXLEY (1894–1963)

In any organization, the org chart tells people of the status of those listed on it. If a guy works for the vice president, he has status. He may not make much money or be very important, but if he works for the VP, he has status. When he moves up a notch on the org chart, he assumes more status. If he was working for a manager and now works for a director, he picks up more status. The pay grade and salary could remain unchanged, but his status increases.

If a Master Corporate Politician is having trouble with a guy, one of the tactics he uses is to remove that status. He doesn't have to cut the guy's pay, pay grade, or anything that involves the idiots in personnel. The Master Corporate Politician can do anything with his org chart that he wants.

I was about to finish an assignment to consolidate two bill-of-material groups into one group. A bill of material is like a recipe, it is all the parts needed to make something—the group is those guys and gals who maintain it. One group was located in the factory, and the other was located at the corporate office. I had to give the leadership to one of the two guys running them. One guy was going to keep his status, and the other guy was going to lose his. I made my decision based on what I perceived as the skills of the two individuals involved. One guy was a technical expert—he knew more about structuring bills of materials and the engineering that went behind them than anyone I have ever met. The other guy was good in dealing with people—he could get people to do things for him, and he got along well with everyone. I selected the last guy.

I wasn't trying to punish the technical guy, but I put him in the people person's org chart. It was where he belonged and where he would do the most good for the organization. The thing I didn't think about was that the technical guy had been a supervisor, reporting to me, and now he was just one of the guys working for the people guy. I had injured him and had not even meant to. He came and talked to me about it, and I pulled him out of the people guy's org chart and left him working for me on my org chart. He did the same thing, helping the people guy get the bills of material correct, but he did it on my org chart. I kept him happy by allowing him to retain his status of working for me, but the work was the same. All policy decisions were made by the people guy, and in one of those rare moments in a Master Corporate Politician's life, an organization chart was accepted by all who were on it and all appeared to be happy.

How would a Master Corporate Politician use this tactic? He would take the guys that he doesn't like and fold them into organizations headed by guys he does like. This would signal the subordinate who has slipped in status that something is coming his way, something bad, real bad. If the loss of status doesn't make him start looking for another job, his ability to get things done will suffer because he now has to go through another layer of management before he can get the kinds of decisions that the Master Corporate Politician reserves for himself. In effect, another layer of management to stall him and get in his way. When he finally gets through that layer of management and gets to the Master Corporate Politician, he will be stalled further. Nothing hurts a guy's pride more than being dropped a level on the org chart. It hurts his feeling of self-worth and makes him feel less important than he did before. In the next chapter we will discuss postponing decisions.

When a Master Corporate Politician wants to punish someone, she takes those things that are working well in the subordinate's organization and gives them to another. When she wants to reward a person, she gives him things that are working well in another's organization. The Master Corporate Politician uses her org chart to reward and to punish.

If a Master Corporate Politician wants to ruin you, she will organize the things that are doing well out of your org chart. You can protest, but it won't do any good. If she wants the good sections working elsewhere, you can scream all you want, but they are gone. She will take all the good sections of your organization and leave you the parts that don't work that well. What the Master Corporate Politician will do for you, to reward you for your efforts, is to give you more sections that aren't doing that well. She will justify it, saying, "You did such a good job with _____ that I want you to square away _____." How do you argue with that? If you are good, then it makes sense. If you are just one of the guys who got lucky, you may have drawn your last ace. If they don't work well, you don't look so good, and before long you are collecting unemployment.

There is no way to stop a Master Corporate Politician, or a human being, from organizing her organization any way she wants to. When you get organized down a level, all I can suggest is that you keep on trying and don't give up. Once you give up or develop an attitude, your days are numbered.

Design a System That Ensures Failure

No failure in America, whether of love or money, is ever simple; it is always a kind of betrayal, of a mass of shadowy, shared hopes.

GREIL MARCUS (b. 1945)

I love this tactic because so many companies do it to themselves already. It is stupidity squared—insanity gone wild. Here's how it works due to the MBAs and their obsession for control. I'll show it to you by example. Here are the steps that were required to get a purchase order placed on an engineering program. My former boss asked me to look into and fix their material-procurement problems. The steps were

1. An engineer determines the need for a part. He fills out a requisition.

2. The chief engineer must approve the requisition.

3. The manager of engineering must approve the requisition.

4. The requisition must go by overnight mail to the corporate office, where it is logged in by the procurement department.

5. The finance department must approve.

6. The program-office people must approve.

7. The quality assurance people need to approve.

8. The requisition goes back to procurement, who load it into the computer. They create the purchase order and depending on the value of the order, must get additional approval.

9. The chief of procurement must approve if at a certain dollar amount.

10. The manager of procurement must approve if at a certain dollar amount.

11. The director of procurement must approve if at a certain dollar amount.

12. The vice president of procurement must approve if at a certain dollar amount.

13. The general manager must approve if at a certain dollar amount.

14. The corporate president must approve if at a certain dollar amount.

Now, I ask you, how many of these fourteen steps are really required? Do you know that if we needed to buy one seven-cent resistor, we needed to go through step 8? I call this control. To spend $.07 we needed the signatures of the engineer, the chief engineer, the manager of engineering, the finance guy, and the program office guy, the quality guy, and then the buyer when she placed the order. Think of it, seven guys approving an expenditure of seven cents. Is that control, or what?

This system was as if some people set out to intentionally make the procurement process impossible, and they did. It was as if some Master Corporate Politician got mad at the engineering department and decided to punish them. I don't think this was the case, but it shows you how if someone had wanted to make it difficult to do something, he could. An interesting observation. The budgets were all overrun. Since so many are signing things, nobody was responsible. Interesting, yes? We had control, but we were out of control.

The Master Corporate Politician defines the procedures that are followed in his organization. If he wants to slow you down or bring you to a dead stop, he can do it with the procedures he enforces. The more procedures, the more rules, the more things slow down. I debate what to recommend to my boss about the fourteen steps for the procurement of engineering parts, but I thought I might just add another level or two or three to the signature process. Shouldn't he (the director of engineering) be signing these things? After all, he is the director of engineering. We had local financial analysts who were charged with keeping track of what's happening. Shouldn't these guys sign off on all expenditures? What about me, I'm a program manager. Why not slap me on signature too? Hell, let's slap the whole damn organization on signature—one hundred and thirty of us. After an engineer gets the one hundred and thirty signatures, then he can send it to corporate for their review and approval.

Let me give you another example of a system that ensured that little was accomplished and ultimately was doomed to fail. Engineering, where I worked, was controlled by the corporate office. In olden days, all engineering was done there. Since the engineers in the corporate office organized (labor union) the corporation has been setting up engineering organizations all over the planet. The plant where I used to work had an engineering department, but they were not allowed to release drawings; they had to be approved by the corporate office. Guess what happened when drawings created by nonunion members from my plant got up to the corporate office to be inspected and approved by union engineers? You got it, when they were looked at, if they were, they sucked and were sent back for revision. Even production-line stopping changes got clogged up in the union/nonunion debacle. Had the union helped the situation? Had management helped it? Both parties created an organization that did not succeed.

How about the engineering-change process? A system in need of serious overhaul. Here's how it worked at another factory where I once worked. Manufacturing could not build something or was having problems doing it due to an engineering problem. They filled out a form called a Problem Report (PR), and it had to be approved by factory management "to weed out the nonessential." If the industrial engineers agreed that it was an engineering problem and "essential," and only if they did, then they created another form called an Engineering Action Required (EAR), which they statused weekly. Yes, we created one form and then copied the same information over to another form, both prenumbered and accounted for. The EAR was like a voucher whereby engineering could work for up to forty hours on this problem. If the engineers needed more hours, they had to ask for and justify why they couldn't fix the problem in forty hours. This was often a bloody encounter between the industrial engineers who worked for manufacturing and the design engineers who had their own vice president. Once a new budget was established for this task, engineering had to report both design as well as financial status on that task weekly until it was complete. If engineering overran the authorization without industrial engineering's prior approval, then the engineering department's budget had to eat the overrun. Hence, tasks were started and then stopped until budget was revised, started again, and then stopped and so on until the problem was fixed—if ever!

Well, you ask, doesn't this seem like overkill? What is wrong with just picking up the phone and calling your buddy Joe over in engineering and asking him to stop by and help you with your problem? It's a small problem and probably won't take Joe more than an hour or so to fix. What's wrong with this? What's wrong is that a long time ago, the manufacturing vice president was afraid that the engineering department would use factory problems to keep his engineers occupied between design jobs, riding the factory when there wasn't anything else to do. He didn't want to pay for idle engineers, or engineers taking two weeks to fix a job that they could have done in one day if they had to. So, what did he do? He established this elaborate system to stop it and created a full-time position on his staff to manage it. He also paid engineering to have one full-time guy on their side of the building to manage it. They now have two full-time people managing EARs, which average about eighty hours a week of real design-engineer effort. If there are no EARs generated, these guys still collect their salaries. Sounds like real good economic sense to me—two people managing the efforts of two others. Or, let's pay for four people so we can get the efforts of two. Or, let's spend $100,000 a year to manage an annual cost of $200,000. Were we idiots, or what? This was a system in serious need of review.

What's the message? If a Master Corporate Politician wants to slow you down, he can do it with the procedures he imposes. How do you fight it? With logic to the upper management. As you can see, I have made fun of the way we did things—it was ridiculous and a tremendous waste of time and people. If the management of my former company could read this, and I hope they will, then this stupidity will be fixed.

Starve the Subordinate to Death

In the Lord's Prayer, the first petition is for daily bread.
No one can worship God or love his neighbor on an
empty stomach.

WOODROW WILSON (1856–1924)

This tactic has been used successfully on me twice. What is it? Simply, it is refusing to staff an organization with enough people to do the job. The guy running the organization is frustrated and unable to accomplish all the tasks that need doing. Given enough time, the guy is replaced because "things just didn't get done." I think by telling you about how this was used on me, you can get a pretty good feel for how a Master Corporate Politician does it.

The first time it happened, it happened for two reasons. One reason was that my functional boss wanted his own person in my slot—I was not one of his guys. The other reason was that my program boss didn't like me and wanted me off his organization chart—I wasn't one of his guys either. At the time I was naive enough to believe if I performed, then my bosses didn't have to like me. Even with that in mind, my situation was not a good spot to be in.

I had taken the organization from a small crew of people up to almost eighty people when the gods (the Master Corporate Politicians) decided that they didn't like me anymore. As people left the organization, I was unable to replace them. The paperwork always seemed to stall in either or both of my boss's office. When I went to try and break it loose, I was told to wait a while and see if I couldn't manage the organization without that replacement. This went on and on and I was about ten heads short of my original staffing level.

Then the bean counters entered and baselined the head-count budget at current levels, less 10 percent. I had to lay off six more guys. Now I was sixteen heads short (20 percent) of the staffing level I needed to perform my job.

Did things not get done? You bet. Did I get caught not doing things? Of course I did, and I was moved to another program of substantially less importance. Did my functional boss give the job to his person? You bet! Did the new guy get the sixteen heads needed to run the organization? Yes, and almost immediately. Did I quit? It took a while, but I found another job.

The second time it happened, it went almost the same way as the first. I was hired to transfer an organization from one part of the country to another. The original organization was to have established long-term subcontracts, and the new organization would have only to administer them. The original organization consisted of about thirty people, and the new organization was supposed to need only five. I knew right up front that five people were not going to be enough, and I covered that with my management. They said, "Don't worry about it—you'll get the staff you need. Try it with the reduced staff, and if you need more, then we'll give it to you." I took over the organization and began to transition.

As the transition was just about over, the management that hired me got decimated. My functional vice president, the guy who hired me, the program vice president, and their boss, the general manager, were terminated or allowed to retire. So much for my promises of staff if I needed it. The new functional vice president believed in making things happen within the budget. Since I was budgeted for only five people, that was all I got. The new functional guy was also a political appointee, a very intelligent and professional man, but not technically proficient. He didn't understand what I was doing.

My new program boss was also a political appointee and he, too, had no clue. *Deja vu?* I tried every trick I could, but neither of my bosses would help me. My staff was working sixty hours a week, and we were losing ground. Did I see the handwriting on the wall? I saw it, and I knew I was dead. I lasted about six months before they demoted me. Did my replacement get the staffing? Yes, and part of it was me.

So, how does it work? The Master Corporate Politician doesn't give the subordinate the tools he needs, yet the Master Corporate Politician measures him to the performance standards as if he did have them. The Master Corporate Politician tells him that if he can't manage the organization with fewer heads, then his replacement will. The Master Corporate Politician keeps on him to meet schedules that are impossible, and every time he fails, the Master Corporate Politician documents it. When the subordinate complains that it isn't fair, the Master Corporate Politician responds with, "Work smarter, not harder." He tells the subordinate that more heads is not the solution to every one of his problems. In time, the Master Corporate Politician will have sufficient ammo in the subordinate's personnel file that even the most people-oriented personnel officer will let him cream the subordinate.

I have also seen many instances where managers starved their subordinates to death because they didn't know what was going on. I'm sure you've seen it too, where they make some idiot the manager because he knows the boss—not because he knows how to do the job. The manager has a good subordinate who is doing the best she can to overcome her boss's incompetence and still get the job done, but the boss is so "out to lunch" that he can't understand the subordinate when she begs for people. The person ultimately fails, and the manager is forced to replace her. You got it, the new guy will get the staff he needs.

How do you defend against this tactic? There is only one defense and I call it Rule #1, it's who you know (page 2). That rule demands that you be one of the boss's guys. In both of these instances, I was not one of my boss's guys. In one instance, I thought it didn't matter, and in the other, my management got shipped to Siberia, and I was left with new guys who didn't want me. It is imperative that you have one of the big dogs standing guard on your career.

How do you defend if you're not one of the boys? I don't know that I have the answer for that. Look at my track record, bosses two, me zero. I have already been ground up twice with this tactic because I wasn't one of the boys. In retrospect, the only thing I think I could have done differently would have been to jump the chain of command and gone up a level or two. To use this tactic, you would have to assess where your boss stood in relation to his boss. He could either be one of the big boss's boys, one of the big boss's subordinates that the big boss is trying to kill, or he could be a neutral figure in the boss's organization. If he is one of the boss's boys, then a trip to see him would be like taking a shower in a Nazi concentration camp. If he is a subordinate living on borrowed time, then it might be wise to join forces with the big boss, become part of his team, and help him remove your boss. If he is organizationally neutral, there would be two possible results depending on your approach.

> *Result 1:* The big boss listens as you describe the impact of insufficient staffing and takes action that gives you more people, but leaves you working for your boss. It would be like taking an antacid for an ulcer—temporary relief only. You may have saved your life for the short term, but it would have made you only more

on the outside of your boss's inner circle. The final result would be more torture, and finally death.

Result 2: The big boss listens because you come armed to the teeth with other things that your boss has screwed up, documentation on his incompetence, and anything else you have on him. You have gone up the chain with deadly intent. The result is more people for you and either a black eye for your boss or his quick assignment to the unemployment line.

Another possible result of jumping the chain is that the big boss now moves you into the free-fire zone because he fears that you will jump him in the chain when the fancy strikes you. Be careful when you use this tactic as it may have some side effects that you won't like. On the other hand, if your boss is using the starvation tactic on you, or any other tactic in this book, then it's only a matter of time until he tosses your butt into the meat grinder.

 # Staff the Subordinate with Idiots

To generalize is to be an idiot. To particularize is the alone distinction of merit. General knowledges are those knowledges that idiots possess.

WILLIAM BLAKE (1757–1827)

The Master Corporate Politician's motto is, "If you decide you have to give him staff, make sure they are idiots." If you can't *starve him to death,* then make sure all the food he gets contains no nutrition. A subordinate who is in the way of the Master Corporate Politician can't accomplish anything if he's got a staff of "1/2-watters." Consider that light bulbs run anywhere from 40 watts to 120 watts—similar to IQ's ability, drive ambition, and results. People generally run the same range. A "1/2-watter" is a person who burns a half a watt at full glow.

This happened to me. I saw it coming, protested like crazy, but I got stuck with a half-watter. My boss was so much smarter than I was, and he decided that I needed some technical help in procurement. He decided I should hire a rookie college graduate with a technical degree, not the seasoned pro with twenty year's experience that could hit the ground running and be of immediate assistance to me. I could train him, my boss told me, and mold him into the kind of buyer that I needed. I would be investing in the future of the company, because in time a buyer with a technical background would be able to hold his own in the technical discussions with suppliers and not have to rely on having an engineer on hand to interpret for him. I responded that 90 percent of a buyer's job is in contractual language and that what little technically he needed to know, an engineer could cover in short order. I told him I needed a seasoned pro, a war veteran who had been there, who had fought the fight and knew how to fight. I needed an ace, not a newbie. It didn't matter—I either took the rookie technical dude, or I didn't get anything. I took him because anything is better than nothing. Big mistake.

My technical rookie turned out to be a disaster. First, I think he took the job only as a way to get into our engineering department. Second, I believe that at that time, he didn't give a damn about procurement. Third, his fuses were stressed to only burn a half-watt, max. He wasn't motivated, or aggressive. I tried working with him, assigned him a senior buyer to mentor him, counseled him that if he planned on staying with my organization, he needed to get his butt in school and pick up a few formal courses in procurement or take a few NAPM (National Association of Purchasing Managers) courses. He didn't do a thing. He did his job, but there was always something lacking—his heart wasn't in it, and the work was always substandard. I couldn't fire him because my boss expected weekly status reports on his progress and his training. My boss wouldn't hear of me firing him—whatever the rookie's problem was, it was because I hadn't trained him right.

I tried to call in a few markers owed me by engineering so they would take him off my hands, but they weren't in the market for any half-watt technical people. They, too, were pressed to fill their openings, and they needed experienced people, not rookies who didn't burn a full hundred watts. "Ask me for anything, Phil," they said, "anything, but taking that guy off your hands. We are so shorthanded now, and so desperate for good talent, we just can't afford for you to off-load this guy on us. Maybe in a few months, but not now."

I finally got another opening, one of my aces moved on to reap a 20 percent salary increase, and when the boss insisted that I follow the path we had blazed with the technical rookie, I told him that I would quit if I had to do it again. No more rookies. We played the game again where I could hire only technical people, or no one, and this time I waited him out. I used the example of the rookie to explain just about every failure I had experienced in my department since he had been jammed down my throat. I told him that all I needed was one more technical rookie and procurement would close down his factory. He wouldn't budge. I then approached every other person at my level, senior staff to the plant manager, and asked them if they would be willing to let my technical rookie work for them. Without exception, even my enemies, none would take him. I even promised to give them the head-count budget, and the answer was the same. With this information, I approached the plant manager and told him that he must either allow me to hire reasonably, or I was going upstairs. He relented; his experiment at my expense had failed.

A good ending for the technical rookie—he turned out to be a first-class buyer. Yes, he did ultimately work out. I would hire this man again.

I watched one man's career slowly sink under the weight of the idiots his boss packed into his organization. The man, we will call him Fred, was a fairly competent individual, but he and his boss didn't like each other—it was obvious to all of us. Fred ran shipping and receiving, and all shipping and receiving departments are vulnerable to attack.

We had just been awarded a large, multiyear contract to supply printed circuit-card assemblies—lots of purchased parts. The purchase orders were released, and parts started coming in by the truckload. Fred's department was staffed to support the production level prior to the big contract, and he asked for help. Since the budget for the new contract had contained five more people in shipping and receiving, Fred was allowed that many. His boss took losers from other areas of the organization and gave them to Fred. The boss's reason for the in-house transfers rather than newhires was that the people were on staff and Fred needed immediate help. He was "helping" Fred by allowing Fred to bypass the hiring process— he got immediate staffing relief. To further complicate Fred's life, the Master Corporate Politician he worked for took several of the key individuals in Fred's organization and promoted them into other positions not working for Fred. Fred was doomed. He had a staff of people who were not trained and, based on their prior employment history, could not be trained. Fred quit, and a new guy was hired who had worked for the Master Corporate Politician in a prior company.

As a Master Corporate Politician, how do you use this information? If you have a subordinate whom you are trying to get rid of, you make sure that only the half-watters are added to her staff. The Master Corporate Politician will make sure that he personally sees all people interviewing for a slot in your organization, and he will veto any that appear to have a spark of intellect or ability. By making sure that all you have are losers, he insures your ultimate demise.

How do you combat this? How do you manage to keep your gorgeous body from being ground into hamburger patties? I explained how I did it, but that may not always work. If the boss is a Master Corporate Politician and using this tactic to barbecue you, then it won't work. What else can you do? You just wait her out—you have to. If you don't, you have an employee/subordinate who is an anchor to your organization's performance, your performance, and your future. Patience. While you wait, every failure to perform is due to a lack of qualified peoplepower. Every missed schedule, every missed due date, every missed anything is a result of the boss not giving you the assets (proper people) you need to perform.

When confronted with why are you all of a sudden failing on everything you do, your response is canned and consistent. "The boss and I can't agree on the type of people I need to do my job. She expects me to meet her standards of performance, but she insists I use her standard in picking personnel. The two don't work together." You say that enough times, and people start to look at the boss. It's an unwritten rule in corporate politics, often ignored by the Master Corporate Politicians, that you have to give a subordinate the tools he needs to do the job, or you can't cream him if he fails. Oh, you can cream him, but it's a lot harder. When a Master Corporate Politician has given a subordinate a full staff loading and he still fails, then no one looks twice when the Master Corporate Politician chops off the subordinate's head due to failure.

Another approach is to always have a stable of your people waiting to come to work for you. I have many people who like to work for me just waiting for the opportunity to come. First, they know my style, what I expect, and they know me—they either like me or they like the way I operate. There are no games played with my people, and they know it. Once in with me, they're in. I use this list of resumes to fill vacancies when they occur, provided the boss will allow it. It's like stacking the deck—a full house of my people, all loyal to me. Ask any Master Corporate Politician and she will tell you the same. Remember the #1 Rule, It's who you know. Whenever the boss is trying to lay off a bunch of half-watters on me, I hold up the resumes of the seasoned cadre who worked for me before, who know how I want things done, who know how to do it, can do it, and want to do it my way, and it is hard for her to say no. I have a track record of success in getting a job done. Let me do it my way, and it will get done. My failures have been with idiot bosses and my inability to deal with them. You can use the last two sentences as a quote, and it may help you with your boss.

Staff the Subordinate with Loyal People

No man can serve two masters.
BIBLE: NEW TESTAMENT. JESUS, IN MATTHEW 6:24

Similar to Staff Him with Idiots, but this is where the Master Corporate Politician gives his subordinates people who are loyal to himself, not to the subordinate. Ideally, it would be nice if the Master Corporate Politician's people hated the subordinate's guts and were the Master Corporate Politician's partners in getting rid of him.

Think about it for a minute—all your boss will give you are people who are loyal to him, his guys. Does Freddy Krueger come to mind? Do you see the knives cutting your flesh? Are you having a nightmare? Yes, it does happen. The Master Corporate Politician who is out to get you may be loading your org chart with his or her people. First, it gives him or her instant, real-time knowledge of what is happening in your sector of the corporation. Second, it gives him or her the ability to change a direction that you have so carefully plotted. You are doomed!

This is a tactic I use, and one that I know has been used on me. I use it because I have a lot of people working for me that I didn't pick to work for me. They either came with the territory, I was forced to take them in, or they were the only alternative at the time. If I were a Master Corporate Politician, and I am not denying that I am, I would be spending every waking minute trying to eliminate or "pasture-ize" these people so they could do me no harm and I could replace them with Phil people—people who like to work for me. But, I don't. I do use this tactic when I know I have a rabid boss groupie.

Rabid boss groupies are like having a stick of dynamite in your hands, and the fuse is slowly burning down to the end; if you don't do something fast, it's going to explode in your face. I use this tactic to maintain stability in my organization and ensure that things get done. I may not be able to control the subordinate, but I can control the Phil people, and control them I do. With my subordinate surrounded by Phil people, he is unable to make a move without me knowing what he's doing. I know more about his organization than he does. He wants to spy on me to my boss? No problem; I know more about what's going on in his department than he does.

I had a three-layer, eighty-head organization working for me. The layer directly below me was staffed with mostly appointees from top management—a kind of reward for loyalty to them, not me. Some of them were of minimal usefulness, but I had to deal with them.

Some were very good and helped me tremendously. They were all very good men in their fields of expertise. Their expertise, however, was not procurement. All were honorable and hardworking, but procurement was not "their thing." Those who were good were very good. The ones who were bad were really useless. Most were not good.

To give you an indication of what we thought of them, we called them Steers. One of my bosses put one of his boys on my org chart, and I didn't know which one of the staff it was, but I knew I was leaking information worse than the White House. My boss knew what was happening long before I could tell him. I knew I was in trouble. I began to try to find out who it was, and I am not sure I ever did. I isolated it down to two of the six Steers, but I couldn't discern which of the two it was. I cut them both out of my life, and the information flow to the boss stopped.

I was fortunate in that my boss was not looking for my scalp—he just didn't trust me and wanted someone inside to keep an eye on me. If he had been trying to kill me, then his Steer would have been like having a group of Special Forces Rangers inside enemy lines. Every move I made could have been thwarted, sabotaged, or destroyed. It took me a year to isolate it down to two of the six guys, and my boss was not trying to kill me. I don't think I would have lasted a year if he had.

If you are being staffed with the boss's boys, then you

need to get busy finding out who he or she is and getting rid of this informer. He or she is a direct pipeline to the boss and is concerned with the boss's interests, not yours.

How do you defend yourself when your security is like a colander, leaking everything you don't want the boss to know? It's simple—you plug the leaks and punish the leakers. Until you find out who the spies are, you run your organization by the book, no deviations, no exceptions. Once you have sanitized your staff, then you can go back to your normal style.

Can this tactic be used as a countertactic? I guess it could. They have double agents, or so I've read. I haven't figured out how to bring a person into my camp when she works for my boss. I have had several spy-guys attempt to get me to try by naming their price, but I never felt I could trust them. The way I perceive it, the boss always seemed to have more to promise than I did, and I could never be sure when he would offer it, and if he did, could I match the offer. I just don't trust spies.

Summary

I have just shown you ten different ways a Master Corporate Politician can destroy your career by using the org chart, who is on it, and who is not on it. The Master Corporate Politician can just assign you nothing to do. Nothing to do and he doesn't need you. The Master Corporate Politician can demote you so low in the organization chart that you will have to have a ladder to get to the surface. He can organize your department such that even with help from the Almighty you are doomed to fail. He might pluck you just one feather at a time until you have no one working for you. He may try to overload you or move you into an organization where you have no background or experience. He may try to humiliate you into quitting by the organization chart he creates for you. He can put together internal systems and procedures that ensure the fastest speed you can move is similar to running in cold molasses—you can't get anything done. He may try to prevent you from doing anything by refusing to give you the staffing you need. Or, he may give you the staff, but they are incompetent and of no value to you. Or, he may give you a few sharks that are loyal to him to help him eat you.

I'm sure there are many more. If you wish to survive you need to know these tactics when you see them and be prepared. In addition to these ten—I know this is possibly becoming redundant, but it's very important—always remember that the astute Master Corporate Politician will use more than one tactic at a time to get you. Consider meat. The cook may pound it to make it tender, marinate it, pat it with a little dry rub, smoke it for a day or two, or he may use all of the above. The Master Corporate Politician may use three or four organizational tactics, a few style tactics, a couple of direction tactics, and throw in a few punishment tactics for good measure. When you have that many tactics being exercised on you at one time, it is difficult to keep your mind focused on what's important. To survive you must maintain the concentration, or the charcoal grill will turn you crispy brown.

chapter 13

Readying the Plan of Attack

A manager's style is how she approaches a problem. It's how she fixes things, or doesn't fix them. It's how she manages. This chapter deals with how a Master Corporate Politician uses her personal style to get a subordinate to do just about anything she wants him to do—even quit. These tactics are useful to the Master Corporate Politician in other endeavors.

Style is defined by the *American Heritage Dictionary of the English Language, Third Edition,* copyright 1992 as (1) the way in which something is said, done, expressed, or performed: a style of speech and writing, or (2) the combination of distinctive features of literary or artistic expression, execution, or performance characterizing a particular person, group, school, or era.

Think about the definition a minute. It means the way somebody does things. In this application, the world of corporate politics, it is the way he gets things done. For the purposes of this chapter, it is the way the Master Corporate Politician is able to destroy a subordinate's career. We cover ten different ways he can do it. The methods range from

225

destroying a subordinate's ability to do her job by dealing directly with her staff, chewing her butt in public, or letting it be known that the subordinate is not to be trusted. It can also be accomplished by putting the subordinate into situations where it is known up front that she will fail—lots of failures must mean the person is a loser. The Master Corporate Politician will ambush his subordinate in front of management, or force the subordinate into an awkward style, and he never helps the subordinate with priority problems. He will nitpick, postpone decisions, or simply ask the subordinate to quit. These tactics are devastating. They have barbecued many a good man and woman.

Deal Directly with the Subordinate's Employees

I assess the power of a will by how much resistance, pain, torture it endures and knows how to turn to its advantage.
FRIEDRICH NIETZSCHE (1844–1900)

This tactic is used by the Master Corporate Politician to destroy a subordinate's ability to get anything done. How so? If his people are dealing directly with the Master Corporate Politician, then why should they bother to deal with him? Nobody wants to work for any more bosses than they have to, and if a Master Corporate Politician gives an employee the opportunity to deal directly with him, then the employee will ignore his boss and do the Master Corporate Politician's bidding. So what happens? The subordinate no longer has control and anarchy sets in.

If a Master Corporate Politician is trying to ruin a subordinate's ability to get the job done, then he may use this tactic. Every time that I have seen it used, it works. I have seen it used inadvertently—it was not the boss's intent to destroy his subordinate—and it works even then. The subordinate is under pressure from the Master Corporate Politician to get a specific set of objectives accomplished, and his people are not working on them. If this doesn't frustrate him to the point of quitting, then the Master Corporate Politician will ream his butt for failing to get the job done, and that may force resignation. When the subordinate complains that he can't get people to work on his stuff because the Master Corporate Politician has his people doing other things, then the Master Corporate Politician responds with, "I pay you to manage those people, and if you can't do that, then what use are you to me?" If that doesn't work, the Master Corporate Politician can always say, "I have to tell them what to do because you aren't directing them the way I want you to." Either way, the subordinate has no defense and must suffer the consequences.

Here's a real-life example of this tactic in action. I was responsible for the production control of a particular product line at a small electronics company, and I worked for the production control manager. There were four of us working for him, one for each product line we had at that time. My manager and the manager of production were always fighting. The production guy accused us of not doing our jobs (getting parts in from suppliers), and as such he couldn't do his, which was to ship product. We knew this wasn't the case; he had plenty of parts. His people kept building crap and quality kept rejecting it. The feud between my manager and him was a hot one.

In a reorganization, the production guy got promoted to director, and my boss now worked for him. The new director wanted my boss out the door, but my boss wasn't about to leave his job. So, how did the new director get him out? He ignored him completely. Every day and sometimes more often, the other production control guys and I were invited to meetings in the director's office without our boss. We were told what to do and how to do it. When we were given directions that were contrary to my boss's direction, the director said, "Don't worry about that, I'll take care of it." It wasn't but about two weeks before we stopped dealing with our boss and did all of our dealings with the director. A month later, my boss resigned.

This story does have a happy ending. I felt sorry for my boss, but there was nothing I could do for him. The man just sat in his office staring at the ceiling. He had nothing to do, or if he did, the director wouldn't let him do it. Every direction he gave us was ignored because we had specific instructions from the director. It didn't take him long before he stopped trying. My boss gave notice and left the company. A few months later, he called me and I joined him at the new company. We both were making more money than before.

I've seen this tactic used many times, and it doesn't take long to destroy the subordinate. In most instances, the tactic is a forerunner to the subordinate's being put on "special assignment." Special assignment is another word for out to pasture. When the Master Corporate Politician feels he has to use this approach to get things done, the days of a subordinate's life can generally be counted on one hand, or something as serious is about to happen.

Another example: the Vice President (VP) of materials was getting his lunch eaten daily by the VP of manufacturing because of shortages. What did the VP or materials do? He took over the shortage meetings from his director, and these meetings became a bloodbath for both buyers and their supervisors. There were several changes in personnel in the materials department shortly thereafter.

Another example occurred when the production schedule kept being missed by the production manager. He had plenty of excuses, most of them valid, but sales were not being made. What did the VP do? You guessed right again. He took over production and like a gardener, he pulled out plenty of weeds, including the production manager.

What do you fight this with? Prayer and divine intervention are the only things that can stop this one. Seriously, this one is tough to stop. It has never been used on me, but I think that if it were, then I would go in and have a heart to heart with my boss. I would ask him what role he expected me to play and let him know that I wanted to be part of his team—any part he wanted me to play would be okay. In the case of my old boss, I think that if he had done that, the director would have been satisfied with a simple demotion down to my level so he could bring in one of his own guys. Consider it as being cooked medium rare, rather than well done.

Chew the Subordinate's Butt

There is no terror in a bang, only in the anticipation of it.
ALFRED HITCHCOCK (1899–1980)

All the management textbooks tell you that you don't jump a guy in public. They tell you to take him to your office, close the door and then do it behind closed doors. Why? First, it's the professional thing to do, and second, it allows the employee to maintain the illusion that he is something other than meat. Having others witness you chewing a guy's butt humiliates him and terrifies the witnesses—it confirms their fear that they really are meat. Armed with this information, guess what a Master Corporate Politician does? You got it, exactly the opposite of what the textbooks instruct.

This tactic just doesn't fit into my personality, so I don't use it. But I have had it used on me many times and have witnessed it hundreds of times. But I did get so angry once that I let my anger get out of control in a meeting and I unloaded heavy on a guy—one of my subordinates. I realized at once that I had screwed up and spent the rest of the meeting apologizing to him. It didn't help; the damage was done. I felt so bad that I took extra precautions with the individual to make sure he was treated fairly as long as he worked for me.

There are some managers who unload on everybody at any time. These people shoot from the hip—they aim and fire in one motion without thinking about it. This tactic is not that. This tactic is one that, to be effective, must be used very selectively. People learn to accept the person who shoots all the time. They realize that it is the manager's way of managing, disgusting, but her style. When you don't unload on people and then there is an occurrence where you do, it is significant. The one time I used it, people were talking about it for months. The employees had nicknamed me the Bear, and they said of the event, "There was bear fur flying all over the place."

Think about this for a minute. When you are scolded, even unjustifiably so, you feel bad. You are humiliated. When it is done in private, the only one to see your humiliation is the guy dishing out the abuse. When it's done in public, you have lots of witnesses, and everyone gets to see your humiliation. "This guy is meat." The subordinate has trouble looking his coworkers in the eyes after that. It's as if he knew he was meat, and worse yet, they knew it too.

So, how does a Master Corporate Politician use this tactic to force a guy to quit. She just uses it. Every chance she gets, the Master Corporate Politician jumps on the subordinate with both feet and makes sure as many people are watching her do it as possible. If the Master Corporate Politician is using the other tactics in this book, there is going to be a "target-rich environment" for the Master Corporate Politician to implement this one.

To defend against it? How about if you carry a big knife and let it be known that the next guy to chew your butt is going to get it stuck in his neck? The only defense is the Martin Luther King, Jr., defense—passive resistance. It won't stop you from being creamed in meetings, but it will allow you to maintain your dignity and hold up your head with pride. If the manager uses it too often on you, the personnel people will get wind of it and they will stop him from doing it. It is done to me occasionally, and I never feel a bit ashamed when it happens. If I deserved the butt chewing, then I deserved it. If I didn't deserve it, then I begin to feel somewhat superior. Passive resistance is the only way to survive. Okay, you're meat—so what!

How do you to turn this into an offensive weapon? As much as you may hate the idiots in personnel, and it seems to me that some (most) of them are, they can be your ally. Abusive behavior by a superior is against the law, and it generally is the responsibility of personnel to monitor the organization to make sure it is not happening. Document the abuses, the witnesses, and when you have a case, go see them, or your attorney. Attorneys love to turn Master Corporate Politicians and personnel idiots into meat—they *really* love it!

Don't Trust/Don't Like

[They] exchanged the quick, brilliant smile of women who dislike each other on sight.

MARSHALL PUGH (b. 1925)

Nothing makes a person want to leave an organization more than knowing that he or she is neither liked, or trusted. It's another form of branding a subordinate as meat.

"You know that I don't like you and I don't trust you." This was said by a Master Corporate Politician to a friend of mine. Just the thought of it sends shivers down my back. It was like a declaration of war. The Master Corporate Politician had told my friend that it was only a matter of time before he would find his career floating facedown in the river.

Why did the Master Corporate Politician say this? I think it was a gamble on his part to short-circuit the process and have the subordinate immediately start looking for a job. It would save them both the anguish of a barrage of tactics and countertactics. It would help the organization because none of the games would have to be played, and the performance of the organization would not have to suffer. A smart move on the Master Corporate Politician's part, or an error in judgment? In my friend's case it was a master stroke. He was gone in less than a month. If the Master Corporate Politician had said the same to me, it might have been a different story. I would have been prewarned and prepared for the onslaught.

Most Master Corporate Politicians never let you know where you stand with them. Why should they? If they give you the impression that you are one of their guys, and you think you are, then you are not prepared if they decide that it's time for you to take up residence in the refrigerated section of the supermarket. Grilling a subordinate is much easier if he's not prepared and doesn't know he is a target.

Perhaps in some ways it was a humane gesture. What? Master Corporate Politicians with hearts? No way, you say. The Master Corporate Politician had told my friend that his career with the organization was over. My friend could stay until the Master Corporate Politician found a way to get rid of him, or he could start looking for a job. That is as humane as you can get if you are a Master Corporate Politician. Why put the subordinate through all the pain? Why put himself through all the pain? It is like being given a layoff notice without a definite time on it.

How do you defend against this? I refer you again to Rule #1 (page 2). If you aren't on the team and can't get on it, then get out before they throw you out. While you are looking for a job, do your best to get on the team. Suck up to the guys who you know are on it and pray that one of them will put in a good word for you with the Master Corporate Politician. If that fails, pack your bags because you are headed for the grinder.

Some Stains Won't Wash Off

Everyone pushes a falling fence.

CHINESE PROVERB

Here's a Master Corporate Politician rule: Anything in your organization that is not doing well, make sure that one of your subordinates (not you) is associated with it. If nothing else, put the subordinate on a committee to fix it. When it fails, then the reason it did is because the subordinate didn't fix it.

My father, when counseling me early in my career about how to deal with idiots, said, "You can't wrestle with a turd without getting some shit on yourself." This is absolutely one of life's purest true statements. Let me translate it for you. If you get in a fight with an idiot, then some of the idiot is going to rub off on you. Or, if you are associated with a failure, then some of the failure is going to stick.

How does a Master Corporate Politician use this to his advantage? He sticks the subordinate of choice into every dirty, nasty little war he is having, particularly those he knows he is going to lose. Every time the subordinate loses a battle, the brown stain becomes more set. After a few lost battles, the stain is permanent—he's a loser! By constantly putting the subordinate in losing battles, he generates an image of the subordinate as a loser. When other members of management see him assigned to a problem, they know the Master Corporate Politician has already written this one off, and they flee so their names are not associated with it. This alone dooms the problem. It becomes so clear, like the grim reaper walking amongst you, that this problem has been decided to be lost. Anyone with fifty watts or more is packing his bags and moving to high ground.

One of the things necessary for a Master Corporate Politician to get rid of a guy is to convince the guys in personnel that the termination is justified. They don't convince easily; they're idiots, remember. When you walk into their office, they won't come to yours, they can't believe you want to make them earn their pay. "How can this be? He or she is such a nice person. Why would you want to fire good old _____." Everybody to them is "good and old." They never met a loser they didn't like. When the Master Corporate Politician walks in with a track record of one failure after another, counseling to correct the substandard performance, and then more substandard performance, they shake the cob-webs and dust themselves off, and you can see some sort of intelligent life behind their glassy eyes—not a lot, but some. They give you all they have.

Once they realize that the Master Corporate Politician has documented proof that the subordinate is not performing, personnel will want to do a minor punitive action, not the full body slam. "Why don't you give him a week off without pay? Tell him that if his performance doesn't improve in thirty days, you will fire him?" By the time the Master Corporate Politician has gone to personnel, the subordinate is already dead—he is only waiting for the death sentence. The Master Corporate Politician has been the route before and knows what personnel requires to can a guy. "Why not give him one more chance?"

I had a boss, the supreme Master Corporate Politician of all time, who got tired of dealing with the people in person-nel. They refused to allow him to terminate a guy who clear-ly, under any rules you want to use, needed termination. His solution? He told the guy on Friday afternoon that effective Monday morning he would be working for personnel and to report to their office. Personnel didn't know what to do with him—why would they, they're idiots. The guy sat there for a couple of days and then stayed home. Personnel didn't claim him so when he had been gone a week, my boss asked per-sonnel to fire him because he hadn't showed up for work and hadn't called in. At this point, the director of personnel got involved, and the employee was given his walking papers.

The point of this section is that if the Master Corporate Politician wants to get rid of you, he will see to it that every-thing associated with your business life is a failure. Once you get a reputation as a loser, then there is no way to escape to another organization within the same company—your only alternative is to hit the road. Remember, brown stain won't wash off.

A lot of Master Corporate Politicians use this tactic to save their own lives. When things start to get nasty and the big dogs are looking to eat someone, the Master Corporate Politician will pick a subordinate to carry her flag. This means that the feeding frenzy will take place on the subordinate, not on the Master Corporate Politician. Whom does she pick? She picks the guy whom she wants to die, or the guy whom she can afford to lose. If you are not on the Master Corporate Politician's team, then you are expendable. Meat.

What do you do if you are the one picked to carry the cross for your boss's failures? Carry it, but let anyone who will listen know that you are only the carrier, not the creator.

Ambush

> For I have sworn thee fair, and thought thee bright,
> Who art as black as hell, as dark as night.
> **WILLIAM SHAKESPEARE** (1564–1616)

This happened to me and started the ruin of my career at one company. We had the customer and both group and corporate vice presidents (all of our company's big dogs) coming in for a program review. We were behind schedule and were not going to be able to make it up. The reason we were behind was that the engineers had been late, were still late, and the production was starting. The design changes were coming in daily, and as the procurement department, we did the best we could to buy the new parts. We were behind, and production was going to be late starting and late finishing. My fault? Not a bit, but as the last organization in the chain of events necessary to get parts to production, we were in the spotlight.

My director did a dry-run program review. I arrived with my charts showing that production was not going to be able to start for three more months and then only if engineering honored their promised engineering drawing release dates. This information was going to cause major problems for my boss as he had been telling the customer that we would deliver the product only a month late. Three months was suicide for my boss. After the dry-run, he called me into his office and we redid my charts. We took out anything remotely close to telling the truth. When we were finished drafting my presentation, he said, "Use these charts and throw those others [mine] away. Don't even bring them with you—I don't want anyone to see them now."

Being a good soldier, used to obeying orders, I did as instructed. When I got in front of the customer and all the company big dogs, they were not happy with my presentation. "You aren't telling us anything. When is production going to start?" I looked to my boss for help; he had put me there with instructions not to tell them anything. He wouldn't look at me. They continued to beat me up, and my boss didn't help me any. I didn't think that I could say, "See that little worm sitting to your right? He's the one who told me not to tell you anything. Ask him all these questions that I can't answer." I didn't, and when the presentation was over, I'm sure that the vice presidents of my company were convinced that I was not the right guy for the position I held. A vision flashed before my eyes of me being tied at the stake and a large group of hungry cannibals circling me, screaming, "We want meat!"

I had been ambushed by my own management. I had been sacrificed to save my boss's job for a few months. When the word did reach the big dogs that we were three months late, guess what reason they were told for our lateness? You got it—Phil let us down. If his organization had come through, we would have made the schedule. Phil didn't last long after that. Phil became the meat.

Another example with similar results. I had just taken over an organization, and it was filled with some fairly aggressive and competent subordinates. We had to make a pitch to the program manager on the procurement strategy we were going to use to win a big contract. I went to my boss with my charts and told him that I planned on pitching the whole thing, but would have each of my subordinates there in case there were any detailed questions. He didn't think that was a good idea. His direction to me: "Let them pitch their own charts, and give them some visibility. The program manager needs to know who these guys are, and it will allow him to get more information than you can give him." Based on his direction, I told my guys to prepare their presentations and that they themselves would give them to the program manager. Since I wasn't giving them, I didn't spend a lot of time on their charts—they modified them to suit their own style. I just made sure that they were consistent with my introduction and summary.

It was a big mistake on my part to agree to this, but I didn't think my boss had moved me to the "kill-at-any-cost" category yet. I was wrong. When the briefing started, I introduced my staff and told the program manager that each guy was going to do his own presentation, and then I would follow and summarize. The program manager didn't want to do it that way. "No, you are my materials manager, you give me the presentation." I wasn't prepared to pitch the charts and I looked to my boss for his assistance. The bastard just smiled at me. I started presenting, and it was obvious that I wasn't prepared. The program manager hit me with question after question, and I had to defer to my staff. Even my boss hit me with a few. When it was over, the program manager turned to my boss, in front of me, and said, "Is this the best you got?" He was referring to me.

That was the first time that this boss had ambushed me. The next time, when we were submitting the proposal, I reviewed the final numbers with him. He was happy and signed the submittal form. It went up to corporate. That Sunday afternoon, I got a call from him. "Phil, come in to the office right now. We have to cut some money out of the proposal, and we have to do it before eight o'clock tomorrow morning." It was Sunday, and I had some friends over and we had been partying. It was not a good time for me to be discussing a procurement budget. I went in anyway.

A supplier's decrement history is a record of proposed versus settlement price. It is used to gauge how much can be negotiated off a supplier's proposal. It assumes past proposals, and the negotiations on them can be used to predict future proposal negotiations. The proposal I had given the corporation contained the supplier's proposal, the supplier's decrement history, and an analysis by my subordinates of what decrement they thought they could get this year, and why. I had already challenged my guys, and we were submitting a very aggressive proposal—a solid, doable, medium-risk, proposal package. My boss took each supplier and decided to challenge me to accept a bigger proposal decrement. I resisted. His response, "I can do this without you, if you want. Corporate wants more. If I do it without you, then you are still going to have to make it. You going to help me or not?" I helped him, and we got to the number that the bean counters wanted. I didn't think I was going to be able to make it, and I told my boss that. "Don't worry about it; I'll help if you need it."

He helped me all right. We won the contract and after the first financial review, the feces hit the fan. I was asked to justify how I could have submitted such low numbers when the supplier proposals and their decrement history indicated that there was no way that I would ever be able to make it. When they talked to my boss, his response was, "See Phil, they're his numbers." The corporate office sent down a team of internal auditors to look into my proposal practices, and when they were done with me, I was done. The corporation won the contract and lost millions of dollars. My boss helped me by pointing the auditors toward me. The numbers were mine, and he was not associated with them in any way.

Ambushed twice by the same guy. You would think I would have learned something the first time. The message to those of you who want to be Master Corporate Politicians, once a sucker, always a sucker. What should I have done in these two examples? In the first example, I should have been prepared to make the presentation in anticipation of the program manager not wanting to listen to a bunch of subordinates. Or, I should have ignored my boss's suggestion and presented it the way I wanted in the first place. In the second example, I should never have wavered off my number. If my boss wanted to cut it, let him cut it all by himself. Sure, I would have had to answer to why I wasn't making the number, but my reason would always be "the boss cut it, ask him. Judge me based on the proposal I gave you." I used this countertactic successfully in another company.

How do you counter a boss out to ambush you? The first time, you will probably get ambushed. If he does it to you a second time, then it is your own fault—you were stupid. When you have a Master Corporate Politician who uses the ambush tactic, you need always to be prepared to be ambushed. Never trust him again—he thinks you are meat and his grinder is turning and waiting.

Force an Awkward Style

He most honors my style who learns under it to destroy the teacher.

WALT WHITMAN (1819–92)

Another tactic Master Corporate Politicians use is to knock a subordinate off her stride. If they have a person who is used to seeing a problem from a global view, she is criticized for not looking at all the detail. If they have a person who manages the details, then she doesn't have the global view. Whatever the subordinate is, is wrong, and she must adopt the other style.

In my career, I have been criticized for both views. The first time this tactic hit me, I was only five years out of college. I had been praised by my previous boss as the only guy on his staff who could see the big picture. My new boss came in, and we didn't get along at all. He was a detail guy and thought anyone who wasn't was a skimmer. I was a skimmer. He called me that one time in a meeting and humiliated me. Looking at the big picture, and not getting swallowed up with the details, was what I thought being in management was all about. Boy was I wrong. Being in management, to this guy, was tending to your own knitting.

About ten years later, I was accused of being too detail oriented. Here's what my boss told me, "You can't possibly manage that much detail—you need to get your nose out of the detail and manage your department." I was managing only about forty people at the time, and managing their activities wasn't that hard, and I needed to know what each was doing.

I hadn't changed my management style for either one of these guys, so it's interesting that they would each see my style in different ways. To survive in their organizations, I had to change, or appear to change, my management style. Did it add to my stress? Yes, it did. Every time I met with them, I had to remember what management style they liked and modify my approach to solving problems to their way of solving problems.

What had each of these guys done to me? They had broken my stride. In racing, you set a stride and you keep it until you reach the finish line. These guys had broken my stride and as such I wasn't able to run as effectively as I would have if I had been able to run the way I wanted. Were they doing it intentionally? I know that one of them was, and the other was just a jerk who wanted me to do it his way. Each made me change, and each was the recipient of less than what I was capable of doing.

This is a minor tactic that adds a little to the Master Corporate Politician's edge when he is dealing with you. You have to deal with him on his terms and in his style. You can't deal in your style with your methods. Sometimes, I find that the only way to get a job done is by using methods that are peculiar to my style—I get things done, one way or the other.

So what do you do if you run into one of these people? What do you do if you have some Master Corporate Politician who is trying to break your stride so he can slow you down just a little? I haven't changed my style since I developed it. I try to give my boss the appearance that I have, but like being ugly, it goes right to the bone. If you want to win, or survive, then you, too, must adopt a style and hone it to where it works for you. If you let a Master Corporate Politician knock you off your style, then he or she has won a small battle in his or her war to defeat you.

Help with Priority Problems

Every decision is liberating, even if it leads to disaster.
Otherwise, why do so many people walk upright and
with open eyes into their misfortune?

ELIAS CANETTI (1905-94)

When you get into trouble, whom do you turn to? You look to your boss to help you. That's his job, helping you out of jams, working the politics, and generally taking care of you. Your job is to be loyal, take care of him, and always be ready to do whatever is necessary to get the job done. Sounds like a marriage.

What happens when you go to your boss asking for help with priority control? You have fifty pounds of tasks and your organization is stressed to handle only a thirty-pound load. Something is not going to get done, and when that happens, somebody is going to get punished. When you go to your boss asking for help, you expect him to tell you what is really important versus what is only important. The difference is that the really important stuff has to be done, and the important stuff can slip if it has to. From your perspective, things are pretty clear—whoever hollers the loudest gets the most attention. From your boss's perspective, he may not care about the screamer. As a smart Master Corporate Politician, you need to know your boss's priorities. If you work his priorities, then you stand an even chance of surviving if those priorities turn out to be wrong.

The Master Corporate Politician will not tell you his priorities. Why should he? If he tells you, you follow them, and they turn out to be wrong, then he is the one who has to pay the price. If anybody is going to be meat in this social interaction, he wants to make sure it is you. If he doesn't tell you, makes you make your own decisions, then when things go to hell, you are the guy who made the wrong decision. Wrong decision means punishment. You get punished, not the Master Corporate Politician. These guys, the Master Corporate Politicians, are not idiots—they don't work in personnel.

What do you do when you have more to do than your organization can handle? You ask for help with priority control. Ask, and record both the asking and the response. If your boss is a Master Corporate Politician, don't count on anything but evasive answers. Don't count on anything. If he gives you a clue as to what he thinks is important, it will be couched in language that you can't use against him. By recording what he said, you will be able to show proof that you were in trouble, asked for help, got none, and then did the best you could. This may save your life, but if there is a failure, you can count on its landing in your lap. You didn't perform, and now you must be punished for it.

Now, for you guys who think you want to be a Master Corporate Politician. This is where the subordinate tries to get you on board with what she is doing. She will try every trick she can think of to get you to sign up to what is going to be a failure. She thinks that if you are a signatory to her failure, you are the senior guy and therefore you should be the one who faces the dudes with the boning knives looking for meat. Under no circumstances should you sign up to a set of priorities that will result in something not being done. You pay these guys to do stuff for you, and if they can't get it done, then as a Master Corporate Politician you have no choice but to get someone who can.

If they want to fail, then let them do it on their own watch, not yours. Failure for a Master Corporate Politician is a death sentence. Master Corporate Politicians do not fail, someone else does. Remember this.

Nitpick

Perfection of means and confusion of goals seem—in my opinion—to characterize our age.

ALBERT EINSTEIN (1879–1955)

Definition: Make the subordinate justify every dime he spends on travel, and question why he couldn't have done it for less. Look at every one of his phone calls and make him justify why so many, why so long, and so on. Punish him for abuse.

This is another minor tactic designed to make the subordinate angry and seek employment elsewhere. When he submits expense reports to the Master Corporate Politician, the Master Corporate Politician asks him to justify every expenditure. Here's an example:

Boss: What do you mean spending $20 for dinner? Wasn't there a McDonald's in the neighborhood?

Subordinate: Yes, but I was eating with my supplier, and he picked the spot. The rules of ethics forbid us from accepting meals from suppliers. I didn't have any choice.

Boss: I think you could have said something. This is way too high. What about these phone bills?

Subordinate: I had to call my wife—she's been sick.

Boss: Why did you have to stay on the line for fifteen minutes. It doesn't take that long to find out how she's doing, does it?

Subordinate: No, I guess I could have done it in less time.

Boss: That better not happen again, or I'll put a letter in your personnel file. You have a charge on here for room service. You know that it costs more to eat in your room.

Subordinate: I wasn't feeling well, so I decided to stay in.

Boss: Stay in and charge my budget more than you should have? What did you order, the most expensive thing on the menu?

Subordinate: Everything is expensive.

Boss: I think that was my point. I noticed that you didn't fill up the rental car before you took it back to the airport. You know it costs about twice as much as local filling stations.

Subordinate: I was running late. If had stopped, I would have missed the plane.

Boss: So? Your disregard for company money is a serious matter. This is the last time, or I promise a letter in your file. A couple of letters, and we will give you a salary-free holiday.

This goes on and on with each expense report, and letters hit the subordinate's personnel file. When the monthly phone bills reach the Master Corporate Politician's desk, the same ritual begins. Why did you call this guy? Why did you talk so long? What is this? Why? Again, more letters. When there are a few letters, the subordinate is given a week off without pay. When he gets back in, the whole process begins again. The subordinate is now afraid to do anything for fear of another reprimand.

When this happens, the Master Corporate Politician has just about won. The subordinate is now in fear of his job, and when that happens, the Master Corporate Politician rejoices. Fear is a very destructive agent on the morale and attitude of subordinates. When a subordinate fears the Master Corporate Politician, the battle is almost over. It's over because the subordinate is afraid to use countertactics—afraid that if he is caught resisting the boss he will be terminated. Subordinates know that after a salary-free vacation, the next step is out the door. Most companies don't give you two holidays before they cream you.

When used in combination with some of the more brutal tactics, this is like icing on the cake to the Master Corporate Politician. While he's hitting you on the left side of the face with one of the other tactics, he's hitting you on the right side with this tactic, or another one. Using more than one tactic is better than using just one. When two or more are used on you, it's like playing chess—you don't know where the next move is coming from or which of your assets is going to be removed. When you are working for a Master Corporate Politician and he wants you gone, be prepared for a whole arsenal of tactics to be brought against you at the same time.

To defend against this, you must document every expense, phone call, fax, or any other expenditure of company funds. This is a burden placed upon you by the Master Corporate Politician who is trying to destroy you. He doesn't have to go through that type of interrogation, but you do. The only way to win the game is to document everything in your diary of record (page 6). When he writes the letter for your personnel file, take the letter and your notes and go see the idiots in personnel. Show them that the letter is not justified and claim that the boss is abusing you. Being the ilk of people they are, those who live in constant nagging fear of lawsuits, they will bring your boss into line.

Postpone a Decision Until It's Too Late

> *Life, as it is called, is for most of us one long post-ponement.*
>
> **HENRY MILLER** (1891–1980)

There are many times when the subordinate needs a decision from her boss. As an example, you have a supplier who is late in delivering. Do we terminate this supplier and go to another? If the boss is a Master Corporate Politician, he may use the subordinate's need for that decision as a weapon against her. How? He will withhold the decision until it's not possible for the subordinate to recover. Take the supplier example. If the current supplier is not delivering, the subordinate generally cannot terminate the order without approval of her boss. So she waits and waits. While she waits, the supplier gets further and further behind schedule. By the time the boss okays the decision to terminate, the time left to get a new supplier producing has been squeezed to where it is impossible for the new guy to perform. The result: production schedules are missed and management comes looking for someone to punish. Whom do they turn into kabob? Now, not only does the subordinate not have the original guy on order, she has a new guy who isn't performing. You guessed right, the subordinate is beheaded and thrown right into the grinder.

I had a similar experience happen to me. I was a procurement manager with an electronics company, and our engineers had designed several of our circuit cards with micro-circuits sold by only one supplier. I knew I was having trouble with this supplier and asked for a redesign to get this guy's parts out of our product. The response from my Master Corporate Politician boss was, "Phil, you just need to go work the problem a little harder. I don't have the money to redesign the product now, and besides it would take us four months to bring another microcircuit house on line. Go work the problem." I went and worked it, but soon realized that my small order wasn't sufficient to really get their attention. I contacted my corporate office, and the corporate vice president of material went with me to visit them. We still couldn't get their attention, and deliveries continued to slip. At the time, the corporation I worked for was huge, and as a corporation we bought millions of dollars of stuff from this supplier. The corporate vice president then issued a corporate-wide stop order—no more procurement from this supplier until deliveries to me were back on schedule. This did get their attention. They negotiated with me and the corporate vice president, we agreed to a recovery schedule, and the stop-work was lifted. They tried to honor their agreement, but when the dust settled, our production schedule took a hit of four months—the same four that I could have had to bring on a new guy. Not only were they late on the initial deliveries, they remained late on the continuing production schedule—every month was a new excuse, a new failure.

Who got punished for the four months? You got it, the author of this book. Who paid the price every month after that? Me again. The word was, "He tried, but he didn't succeed." I did get the engineers the money to redesign our product and take out this supplier's parts, but that didn't help me with my immediate problem. I was able to get the redesign money due to piece-part pricing—other suppliers were cheaper. I got a black eye because my boss would not make a timely decision and let me change.

This tactic was used on me, not necessarily to get rid of me, but because Master Corporate Politicians are reluctant to make decisions. If they make one, and it turns out badly, then they may have ruined their careers. This is what happened in my example. No one wanted to take the risk, so poor old Phil got stuck with the consequences. If a Master Corporate Politician had wanted to use this as a weapon, the results would have been the same, or worse, for me. If my boss had wanted, and he didn't, he could have used this example of my inability to manage a supplier, my inability to support the production floor, and my general lack of competence for the job.

A Master Corporate Politician will use this tactic when he wants to injure or kill a subordinate. There are so many things that require the boss's approval before you can act—it's designed that way to make sure the boss is part of the decision-making process. Here are few examples of how a boss can stall a decision that will hurt the subordinate.

1. A casting vendor needs tooling money immediately so he can get his tools on order. No money, no tools, no product in six months when it's needed.

2. A new engineering design needs to be prototyped to prove the design. It costs money. No prototype, no proof of design, high risk when production begins building an unproven design.

3. You've just won a new contract that requires you to provide black boxes that perform to a specific set of specifications. You have plenty of electrical engineers (EEs), but there is a shortage of mechanical engineers (MEs). You need the MEs to design the housing and make sure you

can handle the thermal temperatures that the electronics are going to generate. No MEs means you are going to have EEs doing ME work, and that is going to be a disaster.

4. You need a new piece of capital equipment to handle the volume in the sales forecast. Without it, you are not going to be able to make and sustain the production rate. The lead time is a year, and you need to order it now. No order means no equipment, which means you will not make the sales forecast.

These are just a few examples of how your boss can screw up your life by not making a timely decision. In each of these examples, the boss will ultimately give you what you asked for, but she will give it to you late, and when it arrives late, you are already meat. If she is seriously trying to eat you, she will make sure that the things you need in life are always late.

Another method a Master Corporate Politician uses to stall a decision is to put you into a loop. You submit something for her approval, and she finds something wrong with it. She sends it back, and you get to redo it. You send it back up, and guess what? There is still something wrong with it. You get it back and you fix whatever it is that the boss didn't like. You send it back up, and it comes back down. This can go on forever. When asked, the Master Corporate Politician will say that you never gave her something she could sign. If you were a professional, you would have done it right. She will sign it, but only after it is too late for your career.

How do you defend against this? I would recommend that you think ahead. I know that to many of you that is almost impossible. You are saying, "Hell, Phil, I can't control what is going to happen to me next week, much less six months from now." They had an expression in flight school that went, "Get your head out of the cockpit and put your mind five miles ahead of your aircraft." There were a lot of pilots who graduated with me from flight school, most of us went to Vietnam, and about half of us didn't come back. I checked into it as best I could, and almost all of the casualties were guys who killed themselves—they did stupid things, or they had their heads stuck in the cockpit. They flew into mountains, trees, or each other. Very few were killed by the enemy; they killed themselves. Corporate politics is the same way—get your head out of the cockpit, or they will carve your name on a granite wall somewhere.

Specifically, know what is coming toward you and take action long before it gets to you. If you know your boss is slow in decision making, start forcing a decision a month before you really need it. If you have to, pad the lead time of whatever it is that you need. If it is really going to take six months for this action to occur, tell the boss that it might take eight months. It might, so you are not lying. Let as many people as possible know that you need the decision and that your boss is evaluating it. Keep the pressure on him. Let him be the meat, not you.

Ask the Subordinate to Quit

> *People react to fear, not love—they don't teach that in Sunday School, but it's true.*
>
> **RICHARD M. NIXON** (1913–94)

When all else fails the Master Corporate Politician, he may come out and ask you to quit. I've done it, and to my surprise, the employee found another job. It works because there is the implied threat that if the employee doesn't quit, the world is going to come to an end for him. If he quits, he can claim he quit. If you fire him, that will be on his record for life and he will have to explain it every time he seeks employment.

What do you do if your boss asks you to quit? I would recommend that you do what he asks. Sure, you can run to the idiots in personnel and complain that the boss is threatening you and that you fear for your job, but if the Master Corporate Politician did it right, then there was no threat. Here's how I do it:

Me: You know that your performance is not up to the standards I expect for this department.

Subordinate: So your evaluations say.

Me: I want you to consider finding a job somewhere else.

Subordinate: What do you mean by that?

Me: We both know it isn't working here for you. I'm not happy with your performance, and I don't think you are either. I just want you to consider a change.

Subordinate: And, if I don't?

Me: You are going to force me to do what I have to do. You know I don't tolerate substandard performance. We can do it any way you want.

I think you get the idea. I let the guy know I am going to grind his bony butt into hamburger if he stays around, but I don't say it—it's implied. Implication is enough with my reputation. Generally, guys don't need to be asked twice.

If you are asked to leave, leave. The boss is being kind to you.

Summary

This chapter just showed you ten different ways Master Corporate Politicians can ruin your day. They may start on you by dealing directly with your employees and cutting you completely out of the action. They may chew your butt in public to brand you as meat so everyone will treat you as such. They may make it clear that they don't like or trust you, which is your signal to find another place of employment. If they make sure you are involved in every failure in their organization, they are halfway to sending you off to the unemployment line. If they ambush you in front of their management, they do so for one reason only—to reduce your stature so they can put grill marks on your flesh. If they won't help you with your priority problems, and they probably won't, you are on your own in trying to figure out what is important. If they nitpick you, they are doing it to further erode your self-confidence. When they postpone decisions until they are life or death for you, then they have a reason and it isn't because they can't make a decision. They might even come out and ask you to quit.

If the boss's objective is to fire you, these are some of the tactics he or she may use on you. Some bosses use these tactics because they are idiots and don't know any better. But if they are being used on you, assume your boss is not an idiot, and that he is doing it to you intentionally. If you assume that he is an idiot, and he probably is (aren't they all?), then if in this one instance he isn't, your body may get an overnight soak in marinade prior to a nice long hickory smoking. Always assume the worst, and then you are prepared for it.

chapter 14

Keep Your Eyes on the Target

If a subordinate doesn't know what is most important, or his employees don't know, then nothing ever gets done. The Master Corporate Politician knows this and uses it to his advantage to stall and then cripple a subordinate that he wants to disappear. If he keeps the troops guessing as to what is really needed or when it is required, a form of corporate anarchy sets in and everyone does whatever he or she wants. If the subordinate is unable to manage his priorities either because he doesn't know what they are, or his boss is always changing them, he will never conclude any assignment in a timely manner. If the Master Corporate Politician clouds the real priorities with false, unimportant tasks, that which must be done is not done. Remember that Rule #2 in corporate politics is *Someone must be punished for failure*. The Master Corporate Politicians who live at the top of the food chain, the ones who run the world, don't care if the person is guilty or not—they want a sacrifice for the failure. *They want meat!* By constantly changing the subordinate's direction, the Master Corporate Politician will obtain any result he wishes from that subordinate.

Rearrange the Priorities

*When people are taken out of their depths they lose
their heads, no matter how charming a bluff they may
put up.*

F. Scott Fitzgerald (1896–1940)

Another name for this is *priority du jour*. This tactic is designed
to insure that the Master Corporate Politicain's subordinate
never gets anything done. Since she can't get anything done,
she must be ineffective, right? If she's ineffective, then the
Master Corporate Politician will document it, and when the
documentation is sufficient, the subordinate is meat.

How does a Master Corporate Politician use this tactic?
Every day, the Master Corporate Politician rearranges the priorities for her. Today, it is urgent that she complete task A.
Tomorrow, task A is secondary, and task B is most important.
The next day the Master Corporate Politician wants her undi-
vided attention on task C. When task A is supposed to be finished, the Master Corporate Politician calls her in and chews
her butt good for missing the schedule. When she complains
that the Master Corporate Politician rearranged the priorities
on her, the Master Corporate Politician tells her, "You're a
manager, and I expect you to be able to work on more than
one task at a time. You are paid to manage those people."

She responds to the Master Corporate Politician, "I can't
because you are always rearranging my priorities on me. I
can't stay focused long enough to finish anything."

The Master Corporate Politician responds, "Precisely.
That is your problem."

There is no way for the subordinate to win the argument.
First, the Master Corporate Politician is the boss, and second-

ly, the subordinate is paid to get stuff done. If she can't, she must be either incompetent, or she isn't working hard enough or smart enough.

I've seen a lot of managers use this approach by accident. They don't keep their goals focused, and as such, every twitch by their management causes them to jump in another direction. As an example, consider a production line. Everything moves down the line. If you try to rearrange the sequence of one order ahead of the others, the others become late just so you can get the one you wanted. The next thing you know, you have to expedite another order ahead in the process because the vice president wants to know why it is late. This causes others to be late, and before long everything is late. People and the tasks they are doing are very similar to a production line. If you just tweak their priorities a little, everything stays on schedule. If you do massive tweaking, everything goes to hell and nothing comes out on time. When a manager, through intent or lack of understanding, starts to tinker with the priority schedule, the organization goes out of control and nothing comes out.

How to you defend yourself against a manager who practices *priority du jour*? Consider a diary of record (page 6). This is a record of every conversation or direction that comes your way. If you record each adjustment in the priority schedule, when you fail to produce as desired, you have a record of why it happened. Also, when the boss starts messing up your life with his constant changes, tell him that if you have to do this new priority, it will screw up the others. Try to show him at the time he does it to you and attempt to get a new schedule on the task that will slip—you need to fireproof him. Fireproofing (page 71) means that the more people you get to agree with a decision, the less heat you're going to receive if it turns out badly. In application, particularly if you're still low on the totem pole, it means getting your boss's prior approval before taking a risky action. In addition, document the conversation. You can show your boss that his directions were the reason you were not able to succeed. This may help you, but don't count on it. The Master Corporate Politician can, and will, always say to you that he pays you to manage the priorities and if you can't do it, then he'll get someone who can.

Countermand Orders

Chaos is a name for any order that produces confusion in our minds.

GEORGE SANTAYANA (1863–1952)

He says go left, and the Master Corporate Politician says go right. He says go up, and the Master Corporate Politician says go down. Before long the poor employees don't know what to do, and then nothing gets done. Or better yet from the Master Corporate Politician's view, the subordinate doesn't know what to do and then nothing gets done. The Master Corporate Politician's objective is the same as all the other tactics in this book, to make selected subordinates ineffective so he can fire them, or they quit in disgust or despair.

This tactic, similar to Deal Directly with the Subordinate's Employees (page 226) is good at ruining a subordinate's self-confidence. When used frequently, the subordinate begins to doubt his ability to make decisions. When doubt creeps in, the guy is ruined. It's the same as being a pilot. If the pilot thinks he might crash, he becomes very cautious, and that kills people. Caution is a good thing, but *very cautious* is deadly.

Every decision will be weighted with "what will the boss say or do." This will cause him to hesitate and postpone decisions. That, too, is deadly to his own self-confidence as well as the confidence others place in him. It's as if the Master Corporate Politician has made him gun-shy, and that's the whole purpose of this tactic.

Most managers countermand subordinate decisions on occasion—it's their right to do so, and they do it. There is the right way, and the wrong way. The right way has you calling the subordinate into your office, closing the door, and telling her that you are going to overrule her. Explain why so that she understands, and if you are trying to save her, let her implement the new direction as if it were her own idea. The wrong way is to ignore the subordinate and issue different orders. When the two orders conflict, the staff won't know what to do, but they do know the Master Corporate Politician outranks the subordinate, and they will ultimately do as the Master Corporate Politician said.

The next thing that will happen is that the subordinate will now start checking all potential decisions with the Master Corporate Politician before she issues any instructions. She is trying to fireproof the Master Corporate Politician so that she won't be overruled. If the Master Corporate Politician lets her get away with it, she has lost the effectiveness of this tactic. *The Master Corporate Politician won't let her!* He will tell the subordinate that those are decisions that should be made at her level and if she isn't capable of making them, then perhaps she's the wrong person for the job. She then will go out and make more decisions for the Master Corporate Politician to overrule.

When the subordinate comes in and tells the Master Corporate Politician that they need to get on the same wavelength, the Master Corporate Politician will agree with her and tells her to get on the Master Corporate Politician's wave-length. When the subordinate tells the Master Corporate Politician that her organization is the laughing-stock of the corporation because she keeps getting overruled, the Master Corporate Politician will agree with her and ask her when she is going to smarten up and do things the way the Master Corporate Politician wants them done. How does the Master Corporate Politician want them done? He will never commit himself, but he wants them done any way that is contrary to the way the subordinate wants them done.

How to you defend against this? Become or find a postal worker with a gun—they know how. I'm not sure even some-thing that drastic can stop this tactic. If your boss wants to deal this hand, then you have to play it. How do you play? You document, document, document. When he overrules you, then adopt what he wants and work as hard as you can to do it. It has to be wrong, or you are really in big trouble. If it is wrong and you do it just as he told you, then when the world comes to an end, and it will, the headhunters will come for him, not you. Don't let him shake your confidence, and try to fireproof him if you can.

Stupid Assignments

> *Reasonable orders are easy enough to obey; it is capri-cious, bureaucratic or plain idiotic demands that form the habit of discipline.*
>
> **BARBARA TUCHMAN** (1912–89)

Want a really good tactic to screw up a guy's priorities so he can't get anything useful done? This is the one for the Master

Corporate Politician. The Master Corporate Politician will have him do stupid things that waste his energies and staff and ruin his priorities. He assigns high priority to things that have no value and makes the subordinate use his energies and staff to accomplish them. The real stuff that has to be done is not done, and therefore the subordinate can be punished.

I was material manager for a large aerospace company and got this one jammed down my throat. I had over a hundred major subcontractors, and my boss decided that I needed to make status charts on each of them and keep them posted in the "war room." Each chart showed the schedule of requirement, and the suppliers' progress to that schedule. Each was accompanied with a word chart that described the product, the supplier, and if they were behind schedule, the reasons therefore. The boss wanted them updated daily. This meant that my subcontract administrators had to call the supplier, check with receiving, mark up the charts, get them typed, review them for errors, and post them in the war room. This took each of my people two to four hours depending on how efficient they were. In a word, a waste of personnel.

I tried to reason with the boss, suggesting that only those critical or behind-schedule suppliers be updated daily, but he wouldn't have it. He wanted real-time data in his war room. I set about to do it, and it took almost a week of effort to get all the charts up to date. I instructed my people to keep them up to date or I would have a one-on-one session with them. They did it, but other things started to slip. After an especially brutal session with my supervisors, wherein I chewed them out with some of my fancy U.S. Army vocabulary, one of my supervisors came to me and begged to be allowed to update every other day. I considered it, and agreed. I would take the risk.

Two weeks passed and my boss didn't notice, but the charts were still taking a toll on my ability to do real work. I

EAT—OR BE EATEN

then agreed to go to once a week on the updates. This, too, was not noticed, so as an experiment, I told them to stop updating altogether. We stopped, and we waited. I knew I would get a butt chewing, but I wanted to know how often the boss actually used the charts. We waited. It was over a month before he found out, and as expected, I got my butt chewed. My defense was that he didn't use them and they were a tremendous waste of effort. He didn't care. He said he wanted it his way, and if I wasn't going to support that, then he would find someone else to take my position.

Bottom line on this one? I was finished with this boss, and we both knew it—it was only a matter of time—I was meat waiting for his grinder. What should I have done? I guess I should have left the updates at the two-week intervals and hoped that I could have gotten away with it. I didn't, and I paid. I should have documented the cost of updating the charts and brought that to the attention of the boss with a "Do you really want to pay this much for real-time information that you don't use but once a month?"

When a boss gets into the mode of assigning you useless things to do to burn up your people's time, it's time to start looking for another job, or another boss. If this one is used on you, there isn't much defense other than trying to reason with him. Each stupid task he gives you, by itself, is not insurmountable, but when all of them are added together they may become a mountain that you cannot climb. Climb, climb, climb—there are lots of others that want *your* job.

Another countertactic that I could have used was to submit to him on a weekly basis how my personnel were was being utilized—quantify how much time was spent on placing purchase orders, how much in resolving quality issues, how much in expediting, and the big number, how much was spent on creating charts. This would have gotten his attention, particularly if that data somehow found its way into his boss's in-box.

Micromanage

People ask the difference between a leader and a boss. . . . The leader works in the open, and the boss in covert. The leader leads, and the boss drives.
THEODORE ROOSEVELT (1858–1919)

Micromanagement is defined as getting involved in everything a subordinate is doing and making every decision for him. The micromanager checks everything the subordinate does and finds lots of errors or flaws with it. The micromanager will make the subordinate give him daily status on everything he is doing and will chew him out because something didn't happen.

Some people do this naturally—it's part of their management style. Some do it occasionally when it is an area where they aren't comfortable with the performance of a particular subordinate, their own grasp of the problem, or for political reasons. For whatever reason, micromanagement is a tool used by the Master Corporate Politicians to help them get rid of someone they don't want in their organization.

Nobody likes to be micromanaged. It indicates a lack of trust, understanding, something. Whatever it indicates, it's bad. Micromanaging allows the Master Corporate Politician, or anyone else in management, to direct every waking activity of the subordinate. Since each activity is being managed and managed in almost real time, it is impossible for the subordinate to do anything except what the Master Corporate Politician wants done. Guess what? Whatever the subordinate does, she does it wrong or to the wrong schedule. As they say in game shows, "Bzzzit, you lose!"

Here's an example of how it was done to me. This was not a malicious use, but one borne of fear by my boss. I have an accounting degree, among others, and I know how to cook a set of books. I was assigned to work as a financial analyst after being creamed by a couple of Master Corporate Politicians. I was working for the director of material. Yes, it was a demotion, and something totally beneath my skill level, but it was a job. It was something to tide me over until I could climb out of the barrel. My new boss was a brilliant man, a Master Corporate Politician with one weakness—he had no head for numbers. He was smart enough to realize that he was weak in this area, so he didn't trust the bean-counter types like me who were supporting him—I think he got screwed to the wall one time by someone like us. He would check my numbers, question the most obvious of numbers, receive an answer, and then send me back to the drawing boards with more "what ifs." I would come to him with estimates to do jobs and he would call in the buyers, the source of the numbers, and we would argue about where it came from, how did we know it was any good, and could we trust the supplier, the buyer, and so on. This guy was afraid of numbers, and I did twice the work I needed to until he began to trust me. Once I gained his trust, the reviews were cursory. In time, he didn't even look at the numbers. He would ask only, "These numbers good?" I would tell him the weak spots, and there are always areas of risk, and he would sign the estimates.

Was I micromanaged? Yes, but in time I overcame the need for the boss to do it to me. I spent tremendous hours sorting the data for him fourteen different ways, confirming that the buyers could get the parts for the prices that they had given me, and other "do-this" type exercises. In time, the boss grew to trust my judgment and relied on me. Once I had achieved this status, a man the boss trusted, I down-shifted and began to enjoy life. I stayed with him for over six years. It wasn't that I liked him, we tolerated each other, but it was a safe, comfortable job that required little effort on my part, and no stress. A great job if you can find it.

Another occasion occurred with less happy results. This time, I was being hunted by a Master Corporate Politician who was looking to take my career and jam it into his food processor. The vehicle the Master Corporate Politician used was shortages. I was the material manager, and he was the plant manager. It started out innocently enough, but turned into micromanagement. The innocence occurred in that I owed him status on the shortages, when I would cure them, and what I was doing to prevent their reoccurrence. I gave this to him weekly. When I fell from his favor, the weekly meeting became brutal. Every shortage was an opportunity for him to ream my butt, and he took advantage of those opportunities. The relationship between us grew more and more strained as the butt chewing continued.

The plant manager decided that I needed micromanaging, and the weekly meetings became daily meetings. In the daily meetings, the tone of the meetings were still hostile, but now the plant manager started telling me specifically what actions he wanted done. He had no expertise in procurement, and some of the direction was harmful, and most of it not necessary. We then would argue. This went on for a week, and then he decided that I should report back to him at the end of the day with a status of the actions he had assigned me. Now I was not only being micromanaged, but

I was spending a large percentage of my time working his assignments and getting ready for the two daily meetings rather than fixing the shortage problem. Recognize this other tactic and how it is being blended in with micromanagement? You got it, the plant manager was also using the Stupid Assignments tactic (page 260). The two-a-day meetings continued with more stupid directions until my staff became totally ineffective.

Did I pay the price for being micromanaged? Yes, a horrible price. Will you pay if a Master Corporate Politician decides to use it on you? Most likely. How do you defend yourself? You have to do what you're told, but you also have to do what you know has to be done. You have to have covered all the bases, or you're going to be a room-temperature carcass. So how do you do it? You go into maximum overtime mode. You make your staff do the micromanagement tasks and also do the ones you want done. It's going to be tough on them, and on you, but until you can get the Master Corporate Politician to back off and try another tactic, this is the only defense.

 ## Summary

There were only four sections to this chapter, but these are some of the most devastating tactics. I have seen more careers ruined by these tactics than I care to remember. This chapter is a meat-grinder's delight. When subordinates cannot determine what is required, they cannot accomplish it and they are vulnerable to the boning knife. If Master Corporate Politicians want to kill you, they will put you into anarchy mode, and you will never get out until they flush you down the com-mode. Without clear direction, the employees will do whatev-er they want to. If the direction is muddied, they will try to follow it as best they can. When it changes daily or hourly (or is stupid), they give up and do nothing. Your only method of survival is to try to maintain a steady course for your employ-ees while you endure the tactics that your boss is throwing your way. As a former boss of mine said, "Phil, if it were easy, I would have given the position to _____."

chapter 15

Drive the Weak into Extinction

All the tactics in this book are punishment in a fashion. They are all designed to impede progress or to stop the subordinate from accomplishing specific objectives. When the subordinate fails, he is punished, ground up, or barbecued. The tactics in this chapter are mostly what I would classify as minor tactics—tactics that by themselves will not kill a subordinate— medium-rare, not burned. But, when they are used with others, these tactics add more stress and make the subordinate's life more difficult. The section on Internal Audit in this chapter is the one tactic that will maim or kill an employee all by itself—it's deadly. The others are like nuisances; they help the Master Corporate Politician achieve his or her objective, which is your demise and his or her dinner. No raises, permanent overtime, no vacations, constant road trips, or long-term assignments out of town will not harm an employee, only make him seek another job.

No Raises

> *However toplofty and idealistic a man may be, he can always rationalize his right to earn money.*
> RAYMOND CHANDLER (1888–1959)

Generally, the manager of a department gets a salary-increase budget. He normally can spend it any way he wants within some guidelines. The textbooks tell you to pass the losers, give small raises to the mediocre, and save the big bucks for the winners. If he isn't told that, then that's generally what he does anyway—it's natural and accepted by all.

The Master Corporate Politician does it slightly differently. Thinking like a Master Corporate Politician, ask yourself why would you give a rogue subordinate a raise? Why would you take money away from those who are still members of your team to give it to guys who aren't? The Master Corporate Politician passes everyone who isn't on his team—period! If you want a raise, you better sign up for life, or you can plan on making the same amount of money you are making now until you retire, if he lets you. What does this mean to those who are part of the team? You got it, big fat raises. Sometimes the raises are twice what the other department guys are getting because their manager tried to do it like the textbook told him to.

As a tactic to get rid of people, this is excellent. Most Master Corporate Politicians use it with a vengeance. They will pass a guy for years, keeping her share of the salary-increase budget to reward his faithful lap dogs. I didn't realize it at the time, but I was the recipient of such patronage. I was getting twice the merit pool percentage every year, and on top of that I was getting midyear advancements. My salary was like a rocket headed to the moon. I spent six years with a company, and my salary more than doubled in that time. Whom did I work for? Right again—a Master Corporate Politician.

If the Master Corporate Politician passes a guy long enough, he will move on. I've done it to a few guys who were mediocre, but not worth the trouble of actively seeking their demise. They didn't cause me any problems, and they weren't part of my team, but they earned their pay. The Master Corporate Politician will never pay anyone but his people. If you get into an organization run by a Master Corporate Politician, then you better join up, or plan on zero pay growth for your natural lifetime.

What does the Master Corporate Politician say to a guy he has passed? In typical fashion, he says, "I'm not giving you a raise this year—you didn't earn it. Your performance wasn't bad enough for me to fire you, but it surely wasn't good enough for me to reward you." When the subordinate disputes this, the Master Corporate Politician responds, "There you go again. One of the reasons you aren't getting any money this year is because you have this attitude problem." If you point out that you worked more unpaid overtime than anyone else in the building, he responds, "If you could learn to get your work done on time like the other guys, then you wouldn't have to be in here all hours of the day. Try to work a little smarter—plan your work."

So will this tactic work? Think about it. If you are not getting a raise and your contemporaries are, are you going to hang around for more abuse next year? Do you go actively seeking root canals? It doesn't take but a couple of passes for you to get the message. As a boss of mine once said, "Tell me five or six times, and I pick it up right away." When it is dealing with your paycheck, you get the message at once.

Is there a defense against this? Sorry, but there's only one tactic. I refer you once again to Rule #1 (page 2). The boss will pay you what he wants to pay you. Most corporations go through a mock evaluation system where the boss and the employee discuss the employee's performance, but it is highly subjective, and if the boss thinks you are a loser, then face it—*you're a loser*. It doesn't matter what you think. If the boss thinks it's true, then by definition, it's true. If you want a raise, then be the boss's guy, or if you work for me, a Phil person.

Mandatory Overtime Forever

> *I have long been of the opinion that if work were such a splendid thing the rich would have kept more of it for themselves.*
>
> **BRUCE GROCOTT** (b. 1940)

The way this works is to give subordinates assignments with unreasonable due dates so they will have to work overtime to accomplish them. Give them assignments on Friday afternoon that you want done by Monday morning. Hold Saturday status meetings.

The Master Corporate Politician has another tactic he can use on you. It's called overtime. You got it, he can overtime you until you either drop dead from fatigue, quit, or seek divine intervention. Either way, he's happy. Refuse to work it, and you are subject to disciplinary action for failure to follow instructions. Again, he's happy. Either way, he's happy and you're not.

Overtime is something that no one in their right mind wants to work unless they have no family, no life, nothing except the job. Fifty hours per week is about all I can handle on a sustained basis. Any more than that and I become tired and my mental sharpness tends to dull. Put me on a sustained sixty-hour week, and my mind is about as sharp as a butter knife. The Master Corporate Politician knows this is true of everyone. He knows that if he has a subordinate in his way, the best way to beat her is to wear her down to where she is not as sharp as she normally is. Dull opponents make for easy victory.

Another use Master Corporate Politicians make of mandatory overtime is that most subordinates hate it so much that they will willingly seek another job to escape it. If the Master Corporate Politician sees that the subordinate hates it, then he will make sure that it is prescribed forever. "Ten hours a day, six days a week. If you are still behind, then I expect you in here half a day on Sunday." That's sixty-four hours a week. Almost anyone can handle that for a while, but when it becomes a steady diet, even the most dull-witted of people start seeking relief.

Another way the Master Corporate Politician gets to you is to come up with assignments late on a Friday afternoon. Yep, he wants it done by Monday morning. Does he really need it then, or is he just screwing with you? You will never know. He wants it Monday morning, and if he doesn't have it by then, he is going to take you to the slaughterhouse and grind you into hamburger. The only way for you to do it is to work all weekend. Guess what? You are going to spend all weekend doing it. Next weekend? If the boss is after you, then count on it. The rest of your life? If he wants you gone, then kiss your personal life good-bye, or leave.

If the Master Corporate Politician is really in a hurry to get rid of you, he starts marrying tactics. This may include giving him stupid assignments, micromanaging by showing up for ten minutes on Saturday afternoon, or possibly rearranging the priorities late on Friday or Saturday so the subordinate has to work on Sunday. The Master Corporate Politician will make sure that the whole overtime experience is unpleasant and unrewarding. Most professional employees don't have to be paid for overtime, and you can be sure that if the Master Corporate Politician doesn't have to pay you, he won't. Consider sustained overtime either a major failure of your management, or punishment, or that someone is looking to nail your taxidermist-prepared head on his cabin wall.

If you have a Master Corporate Politician for a boss, there is no remedy for the direction to go to mandatory overtime or to work all weekend. You don't know if it is needed to do something that really has to be done, or if it is an effort to get rid of you, or your boss. Until you read this, I'm sure you thought overtime was there to actually accomplish something in a short period of time. Yes, it does happen that way sometimes, but not always. If you are ordered to work overtime, then work it. Whenever I am ordered to do that, and it's been years because I don't normally allow my bosses to tell me how to run my organizations, a statement of a friend comes to mind. He was a maintenance engineer who was unionized. He told me the union philosophy in his own words. "Never break a sweat, and don't take a crap on your own time." I take this attitude when ordered to work overtime. If I have to be there, then I will, but don't expect more than about fifty hours of real effort out of me.

Now, let's talk about the most devastating use of overtime control. The Master Corporate Politician controls how much overtime is worked. As you read this book, one of the solutions often offered to counter the Master Corporate Politician is the use of overtime. You put your staff on overtime to keep up with the schedule and work them until they drop or they make the schedule. Well, consider for a minute that the Master Corporate Politician doesn't want you to keep up with the schedule—she wants you to fail. Now what, coach? No overtime, no victory.

I was working for a Master Corporate Politician and he wanted me dead so bad he would have traded the soul of his firstborn child to make it happen. I was keeping up with his tactics by working the crap out of my subordinates—we were on sixty-plus hours a week, but we were keeping up with him. His solution? No more overtime. The company we worked for paid professional employees a straight-time rate for anything over forty-five hours per week. It wasn't bad, and it sure beat nothing. I was now in a position of telling my guys that they had to continue to work for free while the other departments were being paid, or stopping the overtime. I knew that if I stopped, the Master Corporate Politician was going to win, but forcing my people to work for free was just too much—I guess I just wasn't mean enough. I stopped the overtime, and things started to go to hell. I lasted about three more months in that job before I was converted into hamburger.

What do you do when your boss has so many things for you to do that you can't get them done without overtime, and he won't allow overtime? Consider pulling out that straight razor you inherited from your grandfather and cutting your throat—it will keep the pleasure from the Master Corporate Politician. I don't have the answer to this. If I knew, I would still have my old job. In reflection, I have thought that I should have bumped the problem up a level, but my boss was wired solid up the chain of command all the way to the corporate office. I could have gone to my boss and begged for mercy, forgiveness, or amnesty. But as I told you, this relationship had gone to hell and there was nothing going to stop him from watching my head roll into the basket. Like so many other countertactics, the only one that will work is to be one of the boss's people. I wasn't, and I died.

I think that maybe my epitaph should read, "This guy did pretty good considering he ignored his own advice so many times."

Cancel Vacation Plans

Cultivated leisure is the aim of man.
OSCAR WILDE (1854–1900)

This tactic is used by *the* most heartless of the Master Corporate Politicians. It's not like any of us have a heart, but sometimes some of us like to pretend we do. Those that don't even put up the pretense are the users of this tactic. What is it, and how does the Master Corporate Politician use it? It's real simple. The Master Corporate Politician waits until the last minute and then drops an urgent requirement on the subordinate forcing the subordinate to cancel her vacation plans. The subordinate cancels, does the assignment, and reschedules the vacation. When the time comes up again, guess what? The Master Corporate Politician has another urgent assignment forcing a cancellation of the vacation. This goes on and on until the subordinate gives up any hope of taking a vacation and then settles for a day here and a day there.

If the subordinate has prepaid for a trip and there are cancellation fees, what does she do? She eats them. What if she goes anyway and ignores her boss's direction to cancel? Boot Hill Cemetery in Tombstone, Arizona, is full of guys who ignored something they should have paid attention to. Ignore your boss's direction to cancel and you will find yourself canceled. You must do what you are told or be prepared for a prepaid ticket to Boot Hill.

Why would a Master Corporate Politician use such a nasty tactic? He will use it because it is exactly that—nasty. This is a minor Master Corporate Politician tactic, but one that when used with others just adds more zest to a subordinate's desire to escape the Master Corporate Politician's organization. "The bastard won't even allow me to take a vacation."

I have known guys who are on the shit list of a Master Corporate Politician, and they haven't been on vacation for years. A shit list is an imaginary (or real) list of enemies who will die at some point in time—think Richard Nixon. One guy said to me, "Phil, I don't even bother to schedule it now. I know if I do, it will mean a weekend or two of work. If I don't schedule my vacations now, then I can at least keep my workload down to fifty hours." Does this sound like slavery to you? This guy's boss has been trying for three years to get rid of him. The guy is old like me, and finding a job in middle management when you are over fifty is about as likely as winning the lottery.

When combined with other tactics, this is the one that the Master Corporate Politician uses to break the subordinate's back. The subordinate has been looking for such a long time for the opportunity to escape to the real world, and just as it is about to happen, the Master Corporate Politician pulls it out of her reach. It's like the way the military breaks down captured enemies. They hold out the carrot, and just as the prisoner reaches for it, it is moved just a few inches out of his reach. Does it work? You bet your banana. If you take away a person's hope, they fall apart and then collapse. Look at how the military boot camps work. They break down the soldier, sometimes with a great deal of pain, and then they build him back up. The Master Corporate Politician just does the break-down, and then it's out the door. Using the denial of vacation is one of the ways to break down a subordinate.

How do you stop this? Other than Rule #1 (page 2), you can always run and whine to personnel—they have nothing better to do than enjoy your whining. These people are supposed to make sure you get your vacation, but they rarely care. If they do care, they have to buck the Master Corporate Politicians who are running the place, and they never have the horsepower (or will) to do that. Even when they do have the muscle, I've rarely seen them use it. Kiss it good-bye, and prepare yourself for a pleasant (?) slide down the meat grinder.

Road Trips

> He that travels in theory has no inconveniences; he has shade and sunshine at his disposal, and wherever he alights finds tables of plenty and looks of gaiety. These ideas are indulged till the day of departure arrives, the chaise is called, and the progress of happiness begins. A few miles teach him the fallacies of imagination. The road is dusty, the air is sultry, the horses are sluggish, and the postilion brutal. He longs for the time of dinner that he may eat and rest. The inn is crowded, his orders are neglected, and nothing remains but that he devour in haste what the cook has spoiled, and drive on in quest of better entertainment. He finds at night a more commodious house, but the best is always worse than he expected.
>
> **SAMUEL JOHNSON** (1709–84)

In a continuing effort to keep you informed of all the nasty things a Master Corporate Politician can do to you, I present the road trip, business travel, or whatever you call it in your organization. A weapon, you say? It is if you use it the way a Master Corporate Politician does. The Master Corporate Politician controls where her subordinates go, when, and how long they stay on the road. If she thinks a subordinate needs to go visit a supplier, then the subordinate is put on the road. Engineering conference—hit the road. NAPM convention—you're out'a here. APICS convention—be there! Supplier is late—get on the next plane. Possible strike—get there and talk to the union. Supplier bankruptcy—you and the attorney be there first thing in the morning. Tooling problems—get the casting house and the tooling guy together and you be there. There are a zillion reasons that the Master Corporate Politician can put you on the road, and if she wants you there, that is where you will be.

I don't know about you, but I hate to travel. I stay in hotel rooms that are never as comfortable as my home. I am alone and miss my family. I eat alone, I sleep alone, and I am lonely. I don't hear my children fighting, my wife yelling at the kids, or me, and I don't even know which TV channels are which. I know that sometimes I wish for the silence, but when you have it, you miss the noise. I am a big guy, six-four and two hundred and thirty. They always put me in an airplane seat with the overweight wrestlers. It must be standing rule in the airlines—put the big guys together and the shrimps together. For those of you who don't do a lot of travel, it's an adventure. For those of us who do it regularly, it's a pain.

The Master Corporate Politician knows that if you travel a lot, you hate it. So what does she do? She allows you to travel every spare minute of your life. She turns you into a personal hit man whom she sends out to every assignment where she can justify a travel voucher. "You're already out there, so why don't you stop by Los Angeles and see So and So. It will save me the money to fly _____ out there." Another way they suck you in is that since you have to go to Salt Lake, why don't you stop in on Denver, and Dallas, and New Orleans while you're on the road. Since the boss decides who goes, and who stays, guess whom she picks? She picks the guy she hates the most.

The Master Corporate Politician knows when your anniversary is, when your birthday and your wife's birthdays are, when your children are doing recitals, softball, soccer, and just about anything about you. She knows because she is trying to "pasture-ize" you, and that kind of information is useful to her in her quest. When these important dates or family opportunities come up, guess what? She puts you on the road. She knows you hate to travel, and she knows you don't want to miss your child's first communion, or bar mitzvah. She knows you can't explain why you weren't there when your daughter sang a solo, or your son hit the homer that won the game, or your daughter kicked the goal that won the soccer game. She knows this, and she is doing it to you to force you out of her organization.

Why would she do that? Why would anyone be so nasty? In the world of the Master Corporate Politician, winning is all there is. If you have subordinates who aren't 100 percent on your team, pulling for you, you have boat anchors holding back the performance of your organization. Boat anchors have to go. Is it personal with the Master Corporate Politician? I don't think so. She may even like you personally, but she hates your guts professionally. You are occupying a slot on the org chart that could be held by a loyal, do-anything-she-says, do-it-anyway-she-says guy. The fact that you aren't like that, that you have some integrity and question directions makes you a threat and an object to be eliminated.

So why this petty tactic? It is nothing when used by itself. It is a multiplier when used with some of the other tactics in this book. If you are already frustrated with your work, and then the boss turns you into a traveling road show and lets you come home for a short weekend every two weeks, you get sick of it real quick. If there is no end in sight, you start to consider other forms of employment. Petty? Effective? Yes to both.

When the subordinate's wife/husband starts seeking divorce because she/he hasn't seen her/his husband/wife but a few days out of the last six months, the Master Corporate Politician has driven a wooden stake into the heart of the subordinate's career—divorced people (men or women) are always suspect when management considers promotions. The logic goes something like this, "If they can't get along with the one they love the most, their spouse, how can we expect them to get along with an organization that is constantly changing and is filled with jerks like us. We don't need any problems here."

A final advantage to keeping you on the road is that you are not in the office. Yes, you are out in oblivion land—the place where there is no way to defend yourself. When you are gone, there is no one to hold your position in front of the Master Corporate Politicians who rule the world. They assume that since you are not there, you must not be of any significance, and they will take your boss's word on your fitness for any promotion. There are decisions made daily, and if you are not there to present your position, your position is not represented. Guess who will take real good care of your career for you while you're gone?

I know of no way of talking the boss out of a trip unless you want to sacrifice one of your subordinates. You will have to pass the pain down the chain—what is meat for anyway? If you select your own road warrior, then whenever the boss wants something handled on the road, you have a guy—gun—who is already cocked and loaded. Of course you will still have to take an occasional trip; it's your job, but you don't have to spend a career there. Get a road warrior of your own to keep this from happening to you.

Long-Term Assignments

The heart may think it knows better: the senses know that absence blots people out. We really have no absent friends. The friend becomes a traitor by breaking, however unwillingly or sadly, out of our own zone: a hard judgment is passed on him, for all the pleas of the heart.

ELIZABETH BOWEN (1899–1973)

What does a Master Corporate Politician do when he can't get to a subordinate any other way? He puts him on a long-term assignment, preferably away from home. If not away from home, then away from the mainstream organization. The theory behind this is that if he's out of the mainstream, he's out. Promotions, raises, choice assignments, and career-building connections are all lost to the subordinate who is not there to know and act on them. When the guy comes back, he has no allies to help him, and the Master Corporate Politician can put him into a dead-end job where there is no future.

Another thing the Master Corporate Politician uses this tactic for is to destroy a subordinate's marriage. If you keep him or her away from home long enough, then the spouse will make other arrangements. I've seen this one destroy many a marriage. The military has a serious divorce problem, and it's because they send their people away from their families for extended periods of time. When I was going through medical training prior to going to Vietnam, the officer's club at Fort Sam Houston in San Antonio, Texas, was like a smorgasbord for us young, single officers. The feast was the wives of the officers who were in Vietnam. They were bored, and we were exciting. When you keep a subordinate away from his family for an extended period of time either the husband, or the wife, may make other arrangements. A Master Corporate Politician knows this, and if he has a guy whom he can't get to any other way, he will put him on an extended assignment.

But, Phil, can't a guy refuse to accept an assignment? You can refuse, but if you do, then you are no longer part of the team—you become meat if you aren't already. "This guy isn't with our program—we need to get someone else." Refusing an assignment, particularly if you are encouraged to accept it, is like a death sentence to your career. You never know if it is a genuine assignment or just a ruse to get you out of the way so a Master Corporate Politician can put one of his guys in your slot.

Several assignments have led to big promotions. My boss took a temporary assignment and wound up as the director of materials. He was a first-line supervisor and had a track record of success. They sent him on assignment because he was the best the corporation had available at the time. After he was established, he brought me up with him, but I got to take my family. He was on temporary assignment and was gone so long that his marriage fell apart. It worked out for him, I guess, because he met another lady, and as far as I know they are still married after fifteen years. He would have made vice president, but as he told me, "They had a problem taking a first-line supervisor and making him a vice president—it was just too big a jump for the personnel guys." He made vice president about five years later.

Another guy was sent to the same place to get rid of him. He was a manufacturing guy who was in his thirties and all his contemporaries were in their fifties—he didn't fit. In addition to that, he hadn't grown up in the organization, so he wanted to change things—a no-no for the Master Corporate Politicians who hold the power. They wanted him out, and they pushed him into the long-term assignment. He wound up as a vice president, and as far as I know, he and his original wife are still married. Just because they send you away, for whatever reason, doesn't mean the end of the world. It may mean tremendous opportunity.

They tried to do this to me once. I was sent to California for what was supposed to be a thirty-day assignment. Once I got out there, I uncovered a bunch of stuff that got two vice presidents and the general manager creamed. Was I on anyone's hero list? To the contrary. I was on the hit list of every Master Corporate Politician in that division—I had killed their sponsor and several of their friends. What did they do to reward me? They allowed me to stay there. My family was back in Florida, where I was supposed to be living. It went on for a year. I got to come home every two weeks for a weekend, but you can't raise a family, have a love life, and nurture your spouse if you aren't there. They knew that, and they didn't care. They wanted me to have family problems so I would be distracted. I was distracted. I ended it after a year, closing down an operation prematurely to save my family and my marriage. It cost my career dearly.

How do you fight this tactic? First, you don't know if it is a tactic. It may be a genuine opportunity for you. When asked to go, find out what's in it for you. If it doesn't look like much, then tell them you are not interested. They will tell you that you are making a major career error and that they will never ask you again. If there is nothing there for you, then maybe you can see the writing on the wall. One of two things is happening. First, it could be that they are in a bind and have to send someone out there—you are the most available. Second, it could be that you are the only one they have who can fix the problem. It's not likely, but possible.

Internal Audit

All trials are trials for one's life, just as all sentences are sentences of death.

OSCAR WILDE (1854–1900)

A tactic that many Master Corporate Politicians use to eat a subordinate is to allow the corporation's internal-audit department do it for them. All organizations have internal policies and procedures that govern how business will be conducted. The role of internal audit is to make sure everyone is following these rules. They go about life checking organizations to ensure compliance. If they find deviations from the rules, the guy in charge of that organization had better have a damned good excuse, or he's history. Their reports are read by the controller and upper management. When the controller asks why the rules aren't being followed, people at every link in the chain of command are subject to execution.

The Master Corporate Politician asks for the audit. Is this insanity, you ask? No, because he asked for it. The Master Corporate Politician is asking that the internal-audit Nazis review a particular section of his organization for compliance to the corporation's rules and regulations. If he asked, then he will not be punished because the theory is that he suspected violations and was earnest in getting his organization back into compliance. If they just drop in on the same organization because they felt like it, then the Master Corporate Politician and the subordinate are in serious career-limiting danger. When you ask, you are given a get-out-of-jail-free card.

Almost every organization deviates from the policies and procedures occasionally. In the world of the internal auditor, there is no gray—life is either black or white. The organization either follows the rules, or it doesn't—most of the time doesn't count. One deviation can be enough for the management to end your career as the response to the audit report. Management must respond back to these Nazis with why it happened, what is going to be done to make sure it doesn't happen again, and how they punished the person responsible. When internal audit gets the report, if they aren't happy with the response, people really get screwed up. And, they come back again and again. Management always wants internal audit to be happy so they don't have to deal with them.

Internal audit was one of the tactics used to kill a promising career. I was fighting two Master Corporate Politicians, both of whom wanted me dead. I was winning, and there wasn't much they could do to me, or so I thought. I had them stalemated. The next thing I knew, I had a team of internal-audit Nazis. They spent two weeks going over every purchase order my department had ever issued. They found what I would consider a reasonable number of violations, all minor. They also found one violation, a major one.

The violation concerned delegation-of-procurement authority. In this particular job, I had procurement authority up to one-half million dollars. That meant I could approve purchase orders up to that amount, but if they exceeded that amount, I had to get my boss's approval in writing. In this organization, a breach of authority was a serious offense.

The offense the auditors found concerned a supplier who was turned on (authorized) for a million-dollar contract to deliver unique microcircuits. My buyer had gone to negotiate and called me. "I have to turn them on now, or they can't make the delivery schedule," he told me. "Can I do it?" I told him to go ahead, and I would cover him with a letter to the file. I called my boss and told him what I had done, and he said to me, "Do what you have to do. Don't let a few stupid rules get in the way of good business."

This event happened about six months before the internal audit. When the internal auditor asked me how it was that we had a million-dollar purchase order that had been issued without the vice president's approval, I had no answer. I had forgotten about the whole thing, and the buyer assumed that I had approved it and hadn't bothered to write it up and submit it for ratification. I was caught. When I called the vice president, he didn't remember it and told me that even if he had said what he said, I should have submitted the package to him as soon as possible. He was right.

Now my vice president had the task of telling internal audit how it was that one of his managers felt as if he had the authority to spend a million dollars of the corporation's money without the proper authorization. He did what he had planned to do when he asked internal audit to visit me—he pulled me out of the organization and placed me on temporary assignment doing nothing. My career was over in his organization, exactly as he had hoped it would be.

They have an expression in industry—it deals with a thing called the "attaboy." It means good job—way to go. "You did a great job, attaboy Phil." The expression continues: One aw-shit will wipe out a career of attaboys. This aw-shit wiped my slate of attaboys. My careful use of countertactics was not going to save me. I could have tried to sacrifice the buyer who had failed to do what he should have, but I don't think that would have saved me. The boss wanted my scalp, and he got it.

If the organization doesn't have an internal-audit department that is so easily manipulated, or it is just too dangerous to have anything to do with those Nazis, then I have seen Master Corporate Politicians form a group of their own people to go do the same thing. It's like creating an internal-audit group that works for the Master Corporate Politician, is staffed by people loyal to the Master Corporate Politician, and will destroy anyone the Master Corporate Politician wants killed. From the Master Corporate Politician's point of view, it's like having his own storm troopers. These guys go find all the dirty laundry in an organization and report it back to the Master Corporate Politician. The Master Corporate Politician then uses the information to ruin the subordinate's career. To make it appear legitimate, he will have them audit others in the organization, but the reports will always be favorable, or the deviations minor.

A defense of this tactic? As an old production manager once said to me, "There ain't no defense but to have your shit together." That crude way of putting it is the only answer I know. I was able to hold them off with countertactics, but when I failed to have my shit together, they caught me and ruined me.

Summary

As I said in the introduction to this chapter, all but one of the tactics in this chapter are minor and generally are not fatal when used alone. If each is used then they begin to weigh on a subordinate, and he or she will ultimately leave just to escape them. I have known many people who left an organization just because they got tired of working nonstop overtime. I have known guys who quit the first time they were passed at salary-review time. I have seen people get fired because the boss needed them to cancel a vacation, and they wouldn't. These tactics do work, but they are slow killers, like a cancer. Consider the word marinate.

In Conclusion

In the introduction I told you I was going to give you over one hundred tactics that would help you achieve your objectives. If just one of these helped you, or will help you, then you got your money's worth.

Objective: Conquer the Corporate World

If your intentions after reading this book were to rise to the top of the mountain and rule the world, then this is your recipe book. With this book, you now know how to manage a staff, your peers, and your management to get them to do anything you want. Good hunting! You can put this book down for now, but I recommend you read it often to keep your mind open to all the things you have at your command to obtain your will. You have it all, go forth and rule!

Objective: Survival

If you bought this book to save a career, or survive, then reread this book and commit it to memory. I have given you over one hundred ways in which you can be killed. I can't say that I have covered everything that will come your way, but I do believe that I have hit most of them. Reread this book, and reread it often—it will save your life.

In addition to the text of this book, remember that panic kills. When you know your boss is after you, the normal human reaction is to panic. You say to yourself, "Oh, my God! It's only a matter of time until this guy gets me. I'm dead." You're probably right. You know his track record and you know of the bodies buried on Boot Hill by this guy. You panic. You start doing stupid things, which only help the boss get rid of you. You float your resume on the streets, and the boss finds out—he will—and then he tells his management that you're looking. After that, even if things don't derail, your career is slowly sinking. Don't panic.

I spent eighteen months in Vietnam as a medical-evacuation pilot. I had twenty-eight aircraft shot up by the enemy, was wounded twice myself, and had seven of my crew wounded. We survived because I refused that natural human reaction to panic. The closest I ever came to dying was when guys who were flying with me did panic and almost killed everyone aboard the aircraft. I am telling you now that just because a Master Corporate Politician is trying to serve you up for lunch is no reason to panic. This book has given you most of the tactics you are likely to run across and has given you many countertactics. If you panic, the war the Master Corporate Politician has declared on your career is almost over before you even began to fight. With the tactics I've given you, you can stall the end for as long as you have the stomach for the fight. I have been beaten many times, but I knew it was coming, and I fought it inch by inch. I have successfully held off the Master Corporate Politicians for as long as a year—plenty of time to plan a graceful exit. I made some mistakes, and I paid for them. I hope that you can learn from them and avoid the same land mines that I had the misfortune to step on. Remember, panic kills, and patience has won many battles that otherwise would have been lost.

When they come after you, and they will unless you walk on water, plan your defense carefully and use every tactic in this book. Follow my advice and you might survive to senior management. Remember, in the introduction, how I defined management as eat or be eaten? Be the cook, or the menu? Your choice. Good luck.

INDEX